Chasing the Divine
in the Holy Land

Chasing the Divine

in the Holy Land

Ruth Everhart

Wᴵᴸᴸᴵᴀᴹ B. Eᴇʀᴅᴍᴀɴs Pᴜʙʟᴵsʜᴵɴɢ Cᴏᴍᴘᴀɴʏ
Gʀᴀɴᴅ Rᴀᴘᴵᴅs, Mᴵᴄʜᴵɢᴀɴ / Cᴀᴍʙʀᴵᴅɢᴇ, U.K.

Published 2012 by
Wm. B. Eerdmans Publishing Co.
2140 Oak Industrial Drive N.E., Grand Rapids, Michigan 49505 /
P.O. Box 163, Cambridge CB3 9PU U.K.
www.eerdmans.com

Printed in the United States of America

17 16 15 14 13 12   7 6 5 4 3 2 1

Library of Congress Cataloging-in-Publication Data

Everhart, Ruth.
    Chasing the divine in the Holy Land / Ruth Everhart.
        p.   cm.
    Includes bibliographical references and index.
    ISBN 978-0-8028-6907-4 (pbk.: alk. paper)
    1. Christian pilgrims and pilgrimages — Palestine. 2. Christian pilgrims
    and pilgrimages — Israel. 3. Palestine — Description and travel.
    4. Israel — Description and travel.   I. Title.

BV5067.E94 2012
263'.0425694 — dc23

                                                            2012031298

For Doug

Contents

Acknowledgments

WRITING A BOOK is a lot like going on pilgrimage — in one sense one does it alone, but in another sense, the journey is possible only because of the company of fellow pilgrims.

I owe an enormous debt of gratitude to many people, including the following:

Brian Ide, for conceiving of the "Pilgrimage Project" documentary and my fellow pilgrims: JoAnne Bennett, Ashley Griffith, Charlie Barnett, Michael Ide, Jessica, and Shane, and cameramen Michael and John.

The folks at St. George's College in Jerusalem, particularly Dean Stephen Need, who was extraordinarily generous with his time and expertise.

The congregation at Poolesville Presbyterian Church, who encouraged me to find a wider audience for these reflections, and especially to Carolyn McFall, who bid high on the unfinished manuscript at a church auction. Also, many thanks to Vienna Presbyterian Church, which supported the documentary project, especially Ginni Richards.

My writing groups, who read countless drafts of these pages:

- the Writing Revs: MaryAnn McKibben Dana, Carol Howard Merritt, Leslie Klingensmith, Susan Graceson, and Elizabeth Hagan.

- WWW (Women Who Write): Susan Okula, Christy Bergemann, Lygia Ballantyne, Kathy Murray Lynch, and Phyllis Langton.

Deborah Oosterbaan, who helped me write the questions included in the back of the book.

Susan Baller-Shepard, who has been encouraging my writing since that day in the canoe in the late nineties. I can say, without exaggeration, that this book would not exist without Sue's support.

The monks at Holy Cross Abbey, where I wrote first drafts of many of these chapters in silence, under the baleful gaze of those beautiful black cows.

Everyone at Eerdmans, especially my editors, Reinder Van-Til and Mary Hietbrink, whose probing questions made this a better book.

My parents, Nicholas and Joan Huizenga.

My daughters, Hannah and Clara, who gave me a reason to come home.

My husband, Doug Everhart, who said "I married a writer" even when I didn't believe it.

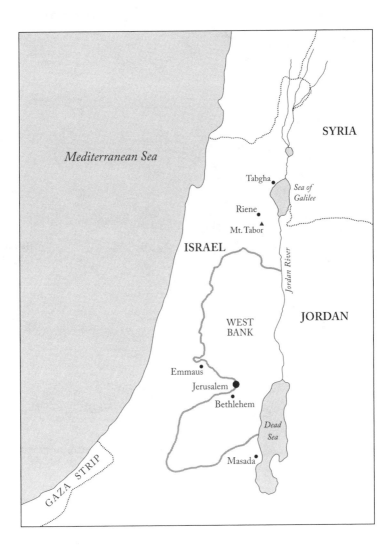

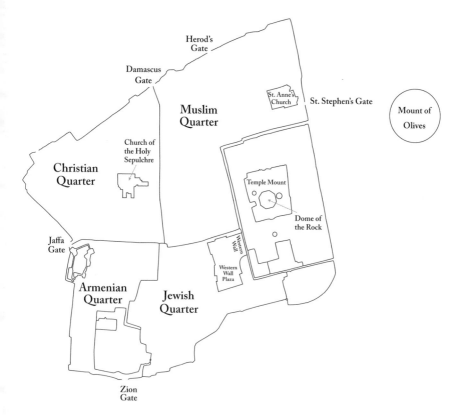

Mt. Scopus

Herod's
Gate

Damascus
Gate

**Muslim
Quarter**

St. Anne's
Church

St. Stephen's Gate

Mount of
Olives

Church of
the Holy
Sepulchre

**Christian
Quarter**

Temple Mount

Dome of
the Rock

Jaffa
Gate

Western Wall

Western
Wall
Plaza

**Armenian
Quarter**

**Jewish
Quarter**

Zion
Gate

CHAPTER I

Uproot Me

I am the bread of life.

JOHN 6:48

T HE MASSIVE DOORS of Saint Patrick's Cathedral make
me feel small, which is probably their intent. If I wanted
to, I could take the time to examine their bronze panels, which
are embossed with religious figures. At least I could look long
enough to find Jesus.

I glance at my watch. In less than three hours I'm to meet my
fellow pilgrims, the strangers I'll be traveling with to the Holy
Land. I'm ready, but I'm also petrified. I'm on that dangerous
threshold — knowing just enough to sense the enormity of
what I don't know.

Going on a pilgrimage supposedly has the power to transform
a person's faith, but how, exactly? And when? And will it hurt?

I could just get the suspense over with. I could walk through
these doors and become a pilgrim right now, a few hours early.
This cathedral isn't on our group's official pilgrim itinerary, but it
is a holy place. Besides that, it holds memories from my teenage
years, when I lived with my family in northern New Jersey. On
visits to New York City we sometimes stopped in Saint Patrick's.
The yawning cathedral space made me feel displaced, which was
unsettling. Mine was a churchgoing family, so sanctuaries usually

felt comfortable. But not this one. I remember the icons — a bloody Jesus and a smooth-faced Mary — and how even those familiar images seemed unfamiliar. It rattled me. If I couldn't connect with Jesus, who was I? It seemed my whole identity might shift. I remember wondering, *So, if I'd been born into an Irish-Catholic family rather than a Dutch Reformed one, would I have become a nun?* The thought had been as thrilling as it was off-limits.

The naïveté of those memories makes me smile to myself as I push against the cathedral door. I couldn't have guessed, back then, that in my quest to find the divine I'd be crossing religious limits — doctrines, ecclesiastical rules, or just the ideas in my head — my whole life. The door doesn't budge. I set my rolling suitcase upright so that I can use both hands, and push harder. Still nothing. Only then does it dawn on me that the door hasn't opened at all during my long reverie. Not a single person has come in or out. I look around and see the sign: USE SIDE DOORS.

Pilgrims may be on a search for the sublime, but they still need to read the signs. I glance behind me, embarrassed, but this is New York City, and people simply stream by, oblivious. I'm grateful to feel invisible as I walk down the broad steps to street level, my suitcase thump-thumping an undignified retreat behind me. I realize I've just missed my chance to examine the great doors' bronze panels. Today won't be the day I find Jesus in them.

The cathedral's side door is swinging constantly on creaky hinges. It's battle-scarred and not nearly as grand as the front entrance. This door is for business, not show. I'm conscious of the size of my suitcase as I navigate the doorway. I packed as lightly as possible, but I can see already that any baggage is too much here. A pilgrim should be unencumbered and nimble. Even ascetic. One tunic was enough for the disciples, right? I pull my luggage across the threshold.

The cathedral is cool and dark after the bright sun of the street. The center nave is shadowy, and stretches high. My eyes follow a marble pillar up to the vaulted ceiling. The surroundings feel like a too-formal friend, but one I'm pleased to see. My love of sacred space has broadened over the years. I may still resist kneeling, and I have never made the sign of the cross, but I love being in sacred space where I might catch the divine presence, lurking.

But this sanctuary feels like a tomb. It must be all the marble, pale and translucent, like it's cooling something dead. The stained-glass windows add a bluish tinge to the air. The only sense of warmth comes from the banks of candles flickering in their red glass holders.

Every time the door swings open, I feel a little sweep of street heat from the warm September day. People enter singly or in clumps: the faithful with their hopeful eyes, the jaded with their shopping bags, the curious with their craning necks. I step into the flow of traffic down the aisle. Side chapels beckon, each one promising a special path to the divine. I look, not at the statues or icons, but at the people who pause before them, who kneel, who light candles with long matches. All these trappings are unfamiliar to me, but I know they're the stuff of pilgrimage. I feel suddenly nervous and hot. I stop and lean against a pillar. The marble is so cool it feels damp. I turn my back to the pillar the way my cat would, pressing the length of my spine along the cool stone, rotating ever so slightly around the pillar.

Candles in a wrought-iron stand come into view, glowing rosily. Two women whisper and grin in front of the candles, their happiness palpable. They're dressed in Bermuda shorts and T-shirts; one shirt proclaims I ♥ NY, and the other has a picture of a lighthouse. The lighthouse woman poses in front of the glowing candles, and I stare at the front of her T-shirt, trying to determine whether the lighthouse is one I know from Delaware or Virginia. Before I can decide, an Asian woman in a business suit steps in front of me, blocking my view. Even though the woman is small and the space cavernous, she is so close that I can hear her impatient exhalation. I glance at her feet, expecting to see high-heeled toes tapping, but she is wearing Converse sneakers. As soon as the women in T-shirts finish their photos, the businesswoman swoops in, lights a candle, genuflects, and leaves.

I feel strangely bereft. Everyone else seems to have gotten what they came for and moved on. What have I come for?

Someone bumps into my suitcase, and I scooch it out of the way. As people file into the pews in the center section of the nave, I realize Mass is about to begin, and I appear committed to it. Well, why not? I trundle my luggage ahead of me down the aisle and, without meaning to, join an extended family, all of them dressed in crisp cotton clothes. I purposely turn into the pew a row behind them to give them some space, but they fill in my pew, as well as the one behind me. My suitcase and I have been absorbed by this large family. I think of the films from science class where an amoeba sends out arms to engulf little bits, to enlarge its mass. At this moment I have become part of something larger than myself.

The priest's voice reverberates in the stone surroundings. I can't understand his words, but when the people answer, "And also with you," I join in before the phrase is done. The woman beside me thunks our kneeler onto the stone floor, and I jump. I feel guilty, caught being a Protestant in a Catholic space. The woman settles herself onto the kneeler.

In front of me the family patriarch is lowering himself slowly onto his knees. His plaid shirt has a Western-style yoke that pulls across his shoulder blades. Beside him, a middle-aged woman whispers in Spanish, her expression tender. When the old man is settled, she cranes around to count her family members. I have the urge to duck so I won't get caught up in her inventory by mistake. But she catches my eye and smiles.

The priest is praying — in English, I suppose — though I can't understand him. I gaze around like a child, counting the pews in their sections, the statues in their niches, the pillars in their rows. Everything is tidy and contained. My eyes travel to the nearest stained-glass window. Instead of trying to decipher the image, I simply stare without blinking until my eyes go milky and the image blurs into shapes and colors. It's hard to do this, not because it bothers my eyes, but because I was trained to approach sacred things in a scholarly way. These bits of stained glass aren't meant to construct a phantasm, but an image that represents a particular biblical text, interpreted through a certain lens at a discrete moment in church history — all of which I must understand. As my veiled eyes let the bits of color revolve into a kaleidoscope, I have a moment of clarity. Maybe my usual approach isn't really the scholar's way. Maybe it's simply a game I play, not to learn something new about the Bible, or faith, or theology, but to feel validated for what I already know. I want to let go of those pretensions as I become a pilgrim. I want everything I think I know to seep away so that faith can become mystery again.

The problem is that I don't know how to do this. Faith has been at the center of my life for so long that it's no more mysterious than, say, my mother's hands, or the steering wheel of my car, or the brown paper sacks I use to pack my daughters' lunches. Faith is part of who I am, used every ordinary day to manage the pieces of my life. What would it be like to step away from everything I know about faith? I've never *not* believed in God, never *not* prayed at a meal, never *not* felt guilty when I did wrong. Isn't that what faith is?

I look around again at this sacred space, so entirely different from the church where I grew up, which was a count-the-cinderblocks box with not a lick of ornamentation. The minister had a broad Midwestern accent even though we were in New Jersey, and his words went on forever — flat and predictable. I'm hearing that voice in my memory when the sanctuary livens with sound. People are saying the Our Father, and I hear my own voice join in. They say "trespasses" while I've finished the quicker "debts." Is it their Spanish accent that makes the voices around me sound more pious than the ones in my memory, or have I encountered a more authentic faith?

I've learned to love worshiping beside strangers, especially when we don't speak the same language. People call that a language barrier, but to me language itself can be a barrier, and silence can be a bridge. Worship without language feels like a way to traverse the division that words can create. Maybe I've been in ministry too long, but I know the limits of words. I'm a Presbyterian, and we're creedal. We are unified by faith in God, yes, but we also subscribe to certain creeds, words people have written about God over the centuries. In fact, we've been known to spend whole centuries arguing over some of those words.

The truth is that, after a lifetime of doctrine, I'm getting tired of words about God. Maybe that's the deeper reason for going on this pilgrimage. I want to find a different way to believe. I want to embody my faith, not just think it. I rest my hands beside me on the pew, palms up — to offer and to receive. Almost immediately I feel a powerful surge of my own unworthiness. It's a familiar feeling, and on its heels comes gratitude for the grace of Jesus Christ. Do I feel these things because of my doctrine, or because I really am unworthy? Whichever it is, I recognize this one-two punch — unworthiness and grace — as the presence of God, which feels sweet, but passes the instant I name it. For an instant I'm angry at my grasping self. If I hadn't tried to put words around it, would the divine presence have lingered?

People are leaving their pews and filing down the center aisle. The priest has moved to floor level and holds a small silver bowl. I know the difference in our theologies of this sacrament, about how Christ is present, and who is allowed to partake of which element, but right now those labels seem like a barrier made of words. Rules. Restrictions. Righteousness. All of which would exclude me. I'm not a Catholic, let alone one in good standing. I'm a woman who has been ordained to administer the Reformed version of this same sacrament — surely that is sacrilege to someone in this cathedral. But might the more important thing be that I'm open to a new experience of this sacrament?

The family around me stands to go forward, and I find myself swept along with them. All right. We're one in Christ, aren't we? This pilgrimage is about hearing the whisper of the Spirit, and the Spirit says *"Come."* Yes, the pilgrimage has begun. I'm leaving home. I'm asking new questions. And God has provided me with the perfect entrance rite, this sacrament of communion with a Spanish-speaking escort.

We surge toward the front. The others open their mouths to receive the sacrament; I hold out my cupped hands. I look around for the cup to dip into, and see none. I slip the flat circle into my mouth and feel it dissolve. I miss chewing a bit of bread, miss tasting the words of Jesus: "I am the bread of life." On the other hand, without the chalice I'm spared the need of pondering blood atonement, a notion that, quite frankly, has been causing me problems lately.

We return down the side aisle. Hovering outside our pews, the family members embrace each other in the Paz de Cristo. I hug the kneeler-thumping woman, then slide into the pew. The old man in front of me sits down laboriously. I squeeze his plaid shoulders from behind. A girl beside him carefully nests a pink vinyl purse in her lap and smiles up at me.

I take my journal from the side pocket of my suitcase and write a prayer:

No address, Dear ____

I seek with all my heart to be open to the leading of the Spirit on this pilgrimage. May my heart and soul bear fruit. May I be good soil for the work of the Spirit. May my life change direction, if need be. May I be willing to bend like a willow in the wind of the Spirit. Change me. Bend me. Break me, if need be. Uproot me. I am yours. Amen.

....

CHAPTER 2

Time like Sand

By faith Abraham obeyed when he was called to set out for a place that he was to receive as an inheritance; and he set out, not knowing where he was going.

HEBREWS 11:8

WHEN I ANNOUNCED to my congregation in suburban Washington, D.C., that I'd been selected to be in a documentary called "Pilgrimage Project," people were excited for me, but also concerned. Was this some sort of TV reality show? Would I get voted off the island, so to speak, kicked out of the Holy Land? It was a reasonable thing to wonder. I couldn't tell them much about the project, not for any sworn-to-secrecy reasons, but because I didn't know much. The filmmaker, Brian Ide, struck me as a person of integrity, and I was drawn to the documentary's twin goals: to lift up the value of pilgrimage, which he described as "faith-based travel," and to follow an intentionally ecumenical group of Christian clergy from different denominations.

Besides those worthy goals, the project appealed to my adventurous side, a side that had been dormant for far too long. Oh, it's an adventure to get married, to get through seminary, to give birth to two daughters, to pastor a church, to raise a family. It's just not the kind of adventure that makes a person update her passport or imagine the smell of olive trees in Palestine.

One member of my congregation asked, apparently in all seriousness, whether I would bring a gun. Another asked, "Isn't it terrifying to think you could lose your life?" I assured everyone that I'd be safe. I didn't say but I did wonder: Is it more dangerous to be a tourist in Israel than to live within striking distance of our nation's capital? Yet the truth was — and still is — that part of me was terrified to take this trip because I *could* lose my life. Not because of bombs or bullets, but because of questions.

There are spiritual questions that I've never gotten around to answering. Not as I grew up in the womb of the conservative Reformed tradition, where everything about faith was warm and safe and reassuring. Not as I studied religion in college, where every question was neatly pegged with an appropriate doctrinal answer. Not as I attended seminary, where the sheer volume of reading material made faith questions easy to ignore. Not as I preached hundreds of times in decades of ministry, where the Sundays marched along relentlessly, each one needing a fifteen-minute sermon void filled.

That backlog of unanswered questions might crowd in on me during this pilgrimage, and what if I can't find the answers to them? What if I misplace my faith? What if I lose it? That is my deepest fear. A preacher without faith is what? The punch line is, of course: Unemployed! But not even that bad joke expresses how I feel. My faith is more than my livelihood. My faith is my life. To lose my faith would be to lose my life.

Let me name a theological problem I've danced around for years, one that starts with the name of the place I'm going to: Holy Land. Why not call it what it is — Land of Holy War? There have been religious wars on this land for millennia, from the ancient stories of the conquest of Canaan, to the Crusades with their forcible conversions, to the warring Israelis and Palestinians today.

Why all the bloodshed? Perhaps the reason is simple. Perhaps it's the other side of the same lesson we teach in Sunday school: God chose a people and gave them a land. That sounds so good if you align yourself with the chosen people. But doesn't this mean that there were others God didn't choose, that there were others who didn't get a land? That makes my brain grind to a standstill.

How can this be true if we call God our Father? I'm not just fussing over gender language here — that's a separate issue. My problem is with this parent language. What parent hands one child a prime toy and ignores the others? Here, have a land! Make it the choice cut, the Chosen Land! What happens to the other children? Wouldn't the Lord of the universe know that choosing one child over another creates sibling rivalry? Parenting 101. No wonder the fighting began. Yes, from the beginning, God created the conditions that forced a breach between brothers: Cain and Abel. Ishmael and Isaac. Esau and Jacob. Joseph and his brothers. If we take these stories at face value, a question seems obvious. Wasn't there a better way to create civilization than pitting family members against each other?

Framed like that, the question terrifies me. I've been taught not to question God, or the words of God in Scripture. I can't imagine the consequences of doing so. My childhood's safe Christianity is worlds away from the Holy Land, a distance you can't measure in miles or time zones. Maybe that's why I'm going on this pilgrimage. It's time to grow up. If I'm going to lose my faith, maybe it's time I just lost it. I picture my parents' faces and feel the prick of tears. They wouldn't understand. But who would? My congregation assumes I have faith figured out. They have no idea what's at stake.

☙ ☙ ☙

We pilgrims are meeting at Saint Bart's Episcopal Church and are supposed to find the filmmaker before we talk to each other. Brian wants to film our initial meeting. The stone steps of the church are broad, forming a plaza that, on this humid day, is spotted with people smoking, or sweating, or speaking intensely into the air — seemingly crazy-person monologues until they turn out to be Bluetooth conversations.

I drag my feet across each broad step, heart pounding, and sneak glances at the faces around me. Is he a fellow pilgrim? Am I traveling to Israel with her? I must find Brian. If the picture on his Web site is accurate, he's under thirty and handsome in a soulful way. I know he has a fire in his belly. Of course, I've never actually met him. It's possible he posted someone else's photo. This entire documentary could be an elaborate scam. He could be a sociopath, lurking . . .

There he is, standing near the columns in front of the church. He's tall and gangly and good-looking. He spots me — I also sent him my picture — and we hurry toward each other, making gestures of recognition, then embrace. My face touches his shirt, and I know that this is real. I'm going to Israel with this stranger. I back away from his shoulder to ask a question but he holds up a finger that signals Stop.

"Can we redo that?" His voice is so pleasant that it takes me a moment to understand. He tilts his head, and I notice two cameramen on the steps below us. "They were both loading film and missed it," Brian says.

The men shoulder large video cameras and point them at us. Reflexively, I look away.

"Just go back there," Brian says, retracing my route with a finger in the air, "then hug me right here — spontaneously, like you just did."

In the plaza people are sweating and smoking and talking into the air like crazy people. But none of them are going to Israel with strangers.

"Ruth?" Brian says.

"You want me to go down the steps. Turn around. Come back up. Hug you. Spontaneously."

He smiles. "Right."

I should have expected this. A documentary. It'll be like a wedding, where nothing counts unless it's captured on film. The cameramen wait, their faces hidden by equipment. Well, then. I'm cooperative — at least I want them to think I'm cooperative. This time I don't eye the faces around me as I cross the plaza. Instead, I feel their eyes on me. I'm not sure whether I should saunter or hurry eagerly. When I reach Brian, I don't know what, exactly, to do. I slide my arms awkwardly around his waist and squeeze briefly.

"That was great." Brian looks across the plaza, where he must have spotted another pilgrim. He says, "I've got to go, but don't follow." A young, dark-haired woman is coming to meet him.

I park myself on the top step of the plaza and get out my journal, hoping that writing will calm me. The two daughters I'm leaving behind are on my mind. The older one is just beginning her first year of college; the other is a sophomore in high school. I write another prayer:

god

> *Dear Lord, watch over my family. Assuage their loneliness. Don't let them feel abandoned. Let this be a positive thing, a time to draw together as father and daughters, an example that personal goals are a worthy pursuit. May this filmmaking venture be a positive thing, to your glory. May my role in it be beneficial. May it positively affect someone spiritually someday. I'll never know who or when or how, but I will trust the power of the Spirit to use our best efforts. Please make me open and articulate — and a conduit of your grace. May my failings themselves be the key to opening someone's heart to you. Please protect me from harm for the sake of my daughters. Please keep them from harm while I'm apart from them. Please, please make this a positive thing. Confirm for me that this was the right decision. I feel the need for that confidence. Amen.*

My eyes rise from my journal — and I'm looking into a video camera. So, according to this new camera-based theology, does this mean that my prayer counts? A few feet away I notice the second camera. Both cameras pivot to focus on a thirty-something man perched farther down the steps. His hair is strawberry blond, and even from a distance I can tell he's perfectly groomed. Two large, wheeled suitcases stand beside him. He glances at the cameras, then at me, and then we both avert our eyes.

Where to escape? The church appears to be open. I notice a sign for a vesper service about to begin and hurry into the sanctuary, where five people are seated. I pick up a bulletin and slide into a pew. Someone produces bulletins for a service with five people attending? They must have astounding secretarial support. The priest begins. He zips along like he's got a taxi waiting. The bulletin helps me find the place in the worship book. Even so, I must gallop to catch up. There's a sung refrain printed in the liturgy, which the priest muscles through without accompaniment. I admire his guts. After the benediction he doesn't even come down from the chancel — just disappears out a side door. Class dismissed. What would that be like, to not shake hands with your people? Seminary taught me that those ten minutes were the most important minutes of my week.

I return to the plaza just in time to see a taxi pull up to the curb. This time Brian runs out to greet the arrival, a middle-aged man, and they cling to each other and laugh. The other pilgrims and I watch the ritual filming of the rolling luggage. This has become something like a wedding rehearsal that's gone on too long.

With the newest arrival in tow, Brian comes up the steps, gathering the rest of us like so many ducklings. There are six of us, and four are women.

"Don't talk yet," Brian warns. "Just follow me." He leads us through a heavy metal door and up several cement stairs. The room we enter is like every other Sunday school room I've ever seen, with laminate-top tables and orange molded chairs. What's different is the Last Supper-style arrangement: two tables pushed together, end to end, with chairs along the far side and at each end.

"OK," Brian announces. "We're waiting for one more, but he's been delayed, so we'll get started. We'll stop and eat when he arrives."

I choose the seat at the end farthest from Brian, and as the cameramen hang a boom microphone over the other end, I feel a gush of relief.

"Tell us your name," Brian says, "and a little about your church."

The youngest woman seems unfazed by the cameras, which astounds me. Her name is Jessica, and she's on the staff of a nondenominational church in Washington, D.C. She speaks with such passion that her slightly frizzy hair seems almost electric. I wonder how many years it's been since I conveyed that kind of energy about ministry. I smooth my hair.

Next is another young woman, and she turns out to be a Presbyterian clergywoman like me. Her name is Ashley, and she speaks with the vivacity of a candidate for student body president. She's married, with one small child. Even before she pulls out the photo, she has my vote for pilgrimage sweetheart.

Someone comes in with pizza boxes, and behind him is the elusive last pilgrim, an African-American man. We pause filming while we help ourselves to slices of New York pizza on cheap paper plates. It's not the meal I'd envisioned, yet it does relax the atmosphere. When we resume introductions, we begin with the middle-aged man whom Brian greeted so warmly.

"My name is Michael Ide," he says.

It's an unusual last name, the same as Brian's, and I think, *Wow, what are the chances?*

He continues, "I'm a Lutheran pastor from Kansas, married, and have three grown sons — "

Brian interrupts: "Which one is your favorite?"

Everyone laughs, and I laugh especially hard, the way you do when you're the last one to get the joke.

We move through the next two introductions. JoAnne is an Episcopalian priest from California who appears to be about my age and is quite down-to-earth. She's followed by the late-arriving black man, who says, "My name is Shane, but I go by ActsNine on stage." I wonder what that means, but he's in a hurry to make something else clear. "I've never been to seminary," he says, cutting his eyes at each of us. "I was converted in prison, and now I do prison ministry." The cameras pan for our reaction. We all wait attentively. I watch Shane's handsome, guarded face and wonder if we'll become close.

The strawberry-blond man introduces himself with a Southern drawl as Charlie. He's attending a Baptist seminary and talks enthusiastically about the large church in South Carolina where he's an intern. The camera then turns to me. Going last hasn't settled my nerves after all. I tell them my name and where I'm from. I explain about my church, that it's tiny and that I'm the solo pastor, half-time. I say the church is healthy — and wonder what that will mean to them.

Last, Brian introduces the two cameramen. They attend the same Episcopal church in Los Angeles that Brian does. I have to focus hard to remember even their names: Michael and John. That makes two Michaels in our group of ten, so one, in my mind, becomes "Camera Michael."

🐦 🐦 🐦

The next morning's itinerary says we'll fly to Tel Aviv by way of London, after some sort of blessing service. Standing in Holy Trinity Lutheran Church, Brian explains that he'd like each of us to lead a brief worship service sometime during the trip, as a way of sharing our faith traditions. He wants us to discuss our differences so we can overcome them. He's all about the ecumenical angle.

"My dad will lead this first service," Brian informs us. "There's an order for prayer, and he's going to pick a Psalm."

Charlie the Baptist asks, "Are we gonna really pray, or use this cheat-book?" He pulls a Book of Divine Worship from a pew rack and brandishes it.

Michael cracks up. He and Charlie were roommates last night and apparently hit it off.

The cameramen need to set up, so I wander away. I'd like to pretend the cameras don't exist. The church is all dark, polished wood and smells like citrus. I climb the stairs to the balcony and see that there's a beautiful organ console with extensive pipes. I immediately think about the organ in my own church, and the repairs it needs, repairs we can't afford. But these are not pilgrim thoughts.

The cameras are ready. "Stand in a semicircle behind the altar," Brian instructs. "Can you look comfortable?"

I want to tell him that I'm doing my best. But there's a camera right there, and, besides that, Presbyterians don't do altars. Have you heard of the Reformation?

Black cord necklaces are laid on the altar, each with a medallion — apparently the image of some saint. After we read Psalm 121 aloud responsively, we're supposed to put the necklaces on each other, though nobody says what they signify.

I wait as Jessica fumbles with the clasp around my neck. The medallion rides on the pulse of my throat, like a talisman. It's my turn to put the necklace on Ashley, and she whispers, "Is this a lucky charm?"

I feel a rush of affection for my Presbyterian sister as I whisper back, "I'm not sure what it is."

JoAnne overhears us. "It's a Saint Christopher. Patron saint of travelers."

After the service we squeeze into a van to ride to Kennedy Airport. Our plane is a huge jet, and we walk further and further back. Our seats are in the second row from the rear wall. We smell diesel and grimace at each other. Maybe that's why the woman in front of me has apparently doused herself with perfume. But we are served free drinks, which I didn't know was standard on transatlantic flights. Outside I quietly order a gin and tonic; inside I praise the Lord.

We are flying east, toward the morning light. Time speeds up as the clock turns back. I imagine I can feel time crumble under us hour by hour as the clock reverses, as if we are barefoot on a beach watching the sand under our toes dissolve with each succeeding wave. But the sand isn't gone, and neither is our day. It's displaced. We will regain it at the end of this pilgrimage. I can't help but wonder: *What will change between this day, which we are losing, and that day, which we will gain?*

We land at Heathrow Airport in London amid chaos. We disembark and wait in a line so endless we can't be sure where it goes. We are pilgrims becoming disoriented to our old world in order to cross a threshold into a new world. In this moment we are in some kind of liminal space between the two. Whatever stratum we might be entering I cannot say. But I can feel my old life slipping away.

Eventually we board a second aircraft as huge as the first.

This time we are seated in the fourth row from the back. Repeat the last six hours. Taxi. Take-off. Diesel fumes. Drinks. Dinner. Time like sand.

CHAPTER 3

Olive Trees and Sparrows

Look at the birds of the air; they neither sow nor reap nor gather into barns, and yet your heavenly Father feeds them.

MATTHEW 6:26

T HE FIRST SHOCK when you walk into the Tel Aviv airport is its size and shine. "Arrival" and "Departure" signs flip over into multiple languages in a futuristic way. It looks and operates more like a movie set than any transportation terminal I've experienced. The second shock is the guns. Guards wearing berets carry long firearms or wear them strapped against their bodies. After twenty-five hours of travel, we're all a little giddy, but the weaponry has a chilling effect.

An eleven-passenger van and driver are waiting, sent by Saint George's College, which is hosting our pilgrimage. Brian hasn't told us much about Saint George's except that it's Anglican and is a host for Holy Land pilgrims based in Jerusalem. He's assured us that we'll be in good hands. Now he informs us that our small group will be joining another larger group of thirty or so. We will fill a tour bus. The words "tour bus" don't sound particularly pilgrimish; we pilgrims frown at each other but don't say anything.

The van driver has long, dark hair and is casually dressed in jeans and an open plaid shirt. He looks proud and handsome. I suddenly realize — why did I never realize this before? — that

I cannot tell a Palestinian from a Jew. Can anyone from the Western Hemisphere tell the difference?

Brian and the cameramen wrestle the luggage and camera gear into the rear of the van. We greet the click of the hatch with applause. Then the ten of us wedge into the three bench seats, with Brian riding shotgun. Maybe "shotgun" isn't the best word. Before we leave the airport, we're stopped by armed men who examine our driver's paperwork. We're allowed to proceed, but a few minutes later are stopped again, and then again. An almost-biblical three times. Vehicles whiz by. The uniformed men aren't interested in us passengers — only the driver. I study his profile. There's a hint of unrest in his chin, which lifts slightly. He never speaks.

We are on our way. Warm, dry air blows through the windows. We pass scrubby hills dressed in shades of beige touched with green. The light is low. It feels as if day is breaking after a sleepless night, but really the day we lost is ending. Eventually we come to the outskirts of Jerusalem, which look like any suburb: residences, office buildings, shops. Lots of cement and little grass. When we pull through a gate and into Saint George's College, a woman emerges out of the dusk to greet us. She introduces herself — a clipped "s" betraying an Australian accent — and reads off our room assignments. JoAnne and I will room together.

We claim our suitcases from the back of the van and tow them across a courtyard, which is suddenly, shockingly, full of people. They all look rested, clean, and crisp. They could even be on their way to church — and it turns out they are. They're Episcopalians on their way to vespers. This is the group we're joining for our pilgrimage, mainly senior citizens wearing no-wrinkle fabrics. They smile sympathetically as we straggle by.

The room JoAnne and I will share has a name, Tabgha, but I'm too tired to be curious. The dorm-style room is spartan but spotless, with tiled floors and tidy twin beds. I want only to take a shower and crawl into bed. I sleep for almost eleven hours.

🐦 🐦 🐦

Breakfast is served in the basement dining room: pita bread, hard-boiled eggs, slices of a mild white cheese, plain yogurt, whole fruit. The coffee is instant Nescafé, which I sip for the sake of the caffeine.

Our documentary group joins the thirty Episcopalians, and all forty of us gather for introductions in the college's one conference room. The air tingles. We're really here, in Jerusalem! Even after so much travel, it doesn't seem possible.

Stephen Need, the dean of the college, leads off. He is a compact man with scholarly round glasses and a crisp British accent. He asks each of us to answer this question in front of the group: Why are you here?

The majority of people are from Canada, and nearly everyone is Anglican. Some people are well-read in Middle East politics, while others are interested in archaeology. Some are biblical scholars and talk at length, while others say little besides their name. I estimate that half the group is over sixty. There are sub-groups from a couple of churches.

"I want to walk where Jesus walked," says Krisha, who recently converted from Hinduism. She is one of the few younger pilgrims, probably in her late twenties. Her sincerity is charming. "I want to see Jesus," she says, "so what better place than the Sea of Galilee? I believe I'll see him there."

In the Reformed tradition we keep a respectful distance from the Savior, and I've always shied away from buddy-buddy talk about Jesus. Who are we, unworthy as we are, to assume we're at the top of Jesus' list? But Krisha's language makes me smile. In my heart I agree that she is bound to see Jesus.

"Pilgrimage is different from other kinds of travel," says Stephen. He quotes: "A visitor passes through a place; the place passes through the pilgrim."* He pauses to let that sink in. "A pilgrim is open to change. The words of pilgrimage are 'May we go home by another way.'" He's referring to the story of the Wise Men, who changed their route home after a dream

---

*Cynthia Ozick, "Toward a New Yiddish," in *Art and Ardor* by Cynthia Ozick (New York: Alfred A. Knopf, 1983), p. 154.

revealed that King Herod was not kindly disposed toward the
baby Jesus. I know the text well: it comes right after Christmas,
on Epiphany, and celebrates the coming of light to the Gentiles.
I'm startled to realize that, by the time I preach that text again,
this pilgrimage — and whatever epiphanies it stirs — will be
a memory.

Now Stephen is saying that pilgrimage is slippery to define.
What do we think it is? Jessica calls pilgrimage a spiritual discipline. JoAnne suggests it's a form of spiritual direction. Stephen
latches on to the difference between those things. A spiritual
discipline is something one engages in, while spiritual direction
is something one offers to another person. This might seem like
quibbling, but I understand what he's saying. It's the difference
between playing the game and cheering from the sidelines. As
a minister, I'm accustomed to the role of guide; but a pilgrim
must be the actual traveler. In other words, a pilgrim must be on
foreign soil metaphorically, if not literally.

Stephen says, "When we seek God, we must start with an
open heart. That may sound sentimental. It's anything but. If
our heart is full of something, we must let that something go."

Someone else suggests that pilgrimage is a way of becoming
rooted and grounded in faith. That phrase is from Ephesians, but
in this context it plays with the physicality of the land. Stephen
nods approvingly and quotes the church father Jerome, who called
the Holy Land the fifth gospel. I think about land as a gospel, a
bearer of God's good news. Stephen says, "It's a surprising land.
Expectations get turned on their heads here. Jerusalem is the
center of the world." As he says this, he spreads his arms wide,
and I'm reminded of the woman who cuts my hair, who made the
same motion when I told her about my plans for this trip. She
had her razor-sharp scissors in one hand as she made expansive
circles: "The pictures from space show a cosmic energy swirl-
ing over Jerusalem. It's the navel of every belief. It's dangerous
because God is dangerous." I had kept a close eye on the blades
of her scissors, circling near my head.

When I come back to the present, Brian is explaining how

the documentary group will fit into the larger group. He assures everyone that the cameras won't get in the way, but at the same time cautions, "If you don't want to be filmed, don't hang out with the documentary group."

"What if I don't know what I want?" asks Marty, an Episcopal priest from Houston who's in her mid-forties, I'm guessing, which makes her one of the younger members of the larger group. She leans forward, forcing her words into the center of the room. "I know how I feel today, but I don't know how I'll feel next week."

Brian replies, "Well, we can edit you out to some degree, but it'll be a problem if you're in every shot."

"Well, I know who this Marty is, right now," she answers in her Texas drawl, "but if Stephen's right, and this pilgrimage changes me, I don't know who Marty might be when this is done."

I glance at Camera Michael to see if he's filming this. Members of our group are shooting glances at each other as if to say, *She's a kook!* But I think Marty is onto something. Maybe the rest of us don't want to admit we're going through a doorway, blind.

"Well, maybe you want to hang back, then," Brian says smoothly. "See how you feel as it goes."

Stephen makes a gesture to conclude the discussion. At last! I feel ready to charge into Jerusalem. I stand up, stretching my pilgrim legs. I just need a decent cup of coffee. Everyone else, however, continues to sit, and Stephen announces, glancing at me, "This first lecture is entitled 'The Historical Jesus.'"

I sit down reluctantly and open my notebook. I doodle a cup of coffee with wisps of steam rising from it.

"Our question is: Who is Jesus Christ for us today? Choosing to focus on this question will be foundational to your pilgrimage experience."

I used to think about that question a lot — Who is Jesus? — but nearly twenty years of ministry have dulled the question's incisive edge. I'm so busy doing Jesus' work (as I imagine it to be) that I assume he and I understand each other. If I'm honest, I know I haven't continued to digest new scholarship as I should do. I have stagnated at the level I preach, which fits into fifteen-minute increments and gives people comfort. Because, Lord knows, we all need comfort.

What do I really believe? Seminary sparked questions I never really answered, and questions have a way of multiplying. Do I acclaim Jesus as a revolutionary, as the liberation theologians do? Do I differentiate between the Jesus of history and the Christ of faith, as Marcus Borg does? Do I reject the historicity of the Virgin Birth, as John Shelby Spong does? I may have one answer for myself, and another for the pulpit. In seminary I thought I would continue this journey of exploration for a lifetime and bring people along with me, but instead I simply call Jesus "Lord" and let my people hear whatever they need to hear.

Stephen is saying, "At Caesarea Philippi, Jesus asked his disciples, 'Who do you say that I am?' The place where that question was asked — Caesarea Philippi, where many gods were revered — mattered. Place always matters." Stephen repeats those three words. "Place always matters."

"Why have we come to Jerusalem to answer the question of who Jesus is?" As if in response, music from the Jewish Quarter wafts in through the open window. It's noon on Saturday. "Shabbat," Stephen explains. The sound fills the room while I hold my breath. Jesus would have responded to that music if he were here, wouldn't he? He was an observant Jew.

Today's music is almost as jarring as yesterday's firearms, a reminder that I'm a foreigner here.

The lecture continues for another half hour, and I'm grateful when we break for lunch. Who knew that being a pilgrim would require so much sitting and listening?

Lunch is a simple meal of pita bread, hummus, yogurt, and various salads. Brian gathers our group to let us know the plan for filming. This evening we'll each give our first on-camera interview about the day's events. "We'll film on the roof, and the night sky will be a perfect backdrop," he says with relish.

I'm already nervous about the camera, and now, stirred by the lecture, I'm full of faith questions. What can I possibly share in an interview? Before I can gather my thoughts or jot them down, it's time to go back to the conference room.

"A pilgrimage is about both past and present. We dig up the past to interpret the present." Stephen lists nine major archaeological finds that we'll see: ossuaries, the Pontius Pilate stone, the Old City, Capernaum, Qumran, Sepphoris. . . . Though I'm writing as fast as I can, I cannot catch them all. Without pausing, he lists more concepts to keep in mind on this quest for the historical Jesus. Jesus was a Jew, so root him in the Judaism of his day. Consider whether he thought of himself as a political figure. Was he a Zealot? Get a sense of his physical, natural world. Always ask yourself about his social world. Was Jesus a wisdom teacher?

I feel cast adrift on a sea of questions and am ready to pick up a paddle. But will I dare to digest and preach whatever I learn on this pilgrimage?

"A pilgrimage is like looking down a well," Stephen says. "You look down history, and you find that you are confronted with yourself."

JoAnne mentions the myth of Narcissus — whose punishment from the gods was to fall in love with his own reflected image — and the group tosses that around. Stephen suggests that we are called to become so focused on Jesus that when we look at ourselves, we see his face reflected. This stops me. I know my face belongs to a redeemed sinner. I have never thought it might reflect Christ.

We haven't seen a single site and already I feel overloaded.

We board a bus, filling every seat, and are asked to "buddy up." My seatmate is Kyle, a tall Anglican priest from British Columbia. Kyle is probably about my age, although prematurely white-haired.

"I'm just going to ask you," I say, "because I should know this. What's the difference between Anglican and Episcopalian?"

"'Episcopal' is the name for the Anglican Church in the United States," he answers.

"That's it? Well, that clears up a whole lot of confusion."

"We Anglicans aim to confuse," Kyle says, "so we can un-
confuse you later." He tells me that he's at the end of a three-
month sabbatical; this pilgrimage is the final segment. I ask him
about his travels, and what the highlight has been so far.

"A week of silent retreat at a monastery in Belgium. Didn't
speak a word the whole week, and at supper every night a monk
set a stein of beer in front of me — and a hunk of this delicious
white cheese."

"So you're saying religious experience comes down to menu?"
He nods. "Beats words, anyway."

While the bus lurches along, Stephen gets on a microphone
and supplies background facts, which I dutifully record. In the
nineteenth century BCE, Jerusalem originated as the city of Salem,
possibly named after a pre-biblical god of peace. Its other name,
Zion, is from the Hebrew *tsia*, meaning "thirsty" or "dry." This is
a desert city built over a water source.

🐦 🐦 🐦

At Mount Scopus, our first destination, it takes ten minutes
for the group to disembark. Somehow I didn't think a pilgrimage would involve quite so many people moving quite so slowly.
Facing east, we look across to the West Bank of the Jordan River.
Two types of architecture are noticeable, even from a distance.
The utilitarian high-rises are Palestinian housing, while the picturesque red-tiled roofs belong to an Israeli settlement. I study
this, grateful that someone has given me the eyes to comprehend what I'm seeing. In the distance is the Rift Valley, which
stretches south to the Dead Sea, its lowest spot. Someone asks
about deserts, and Stephen refers to three of them: the Judean
desert, which surrounds Jerusalem; the Negev to the south; and
beyond that, the Sinai. All three deserts are hilly, with different
levels of vegetation and rainfall. The Judean desert has the most
plant life. Looking at the scrubby growth, I see that a desert is
more than a pile of sand. I haven't paid enough attention to the

different deserts and wilderness in Scripture, ignorantly picturing them all as wasteland.

We turn west, facing Jerusalem, and then look to the south, at King David's City. This is a small archaeological site outside Jerusalem's southern wall, which once contained the original spring. "Notice the water," Stephen says, with his weighted voice. I crane to look for the water, but all that's visible is dust and stone. Someone asks about how the water is routed now, but I have reached saturation on talk about this Holy Land. I'm like a thirsty kid touring the Hoover Dam; I just want to find a fountain.

I glance over my shoulder and notice an olive tree right behind me. I casually back up, then slip underneath the tree's branches. I can hear Stephen talking, saying things I should write down, facts that a preacher should know. But I've never seen an olive tree before. The branches are dense with leaves, the little olives tight and green. I imagine Jesus sitting beneath an olive tree exactly like this one. What did he think about when he looked at olives on a branch? I wish he were here right now. A pair of sparrows fly among the branches. The words of Jesus come to me: "Look at the birds of the air. They neither sow nor reap nor gather into barns, and yet your heavenly Father feeds them." I stay enveloped by the olive tree while Stephen continues to talk. Look at the birds of the air. They neither lecture nor listen nor take copious notes, and yet your heavenly Father feeds them.

Eventually I slip out of the tree's embrace. Stephen is pointing out Jerusalem's Golden Gate with its double arch, now sealed, and he gives its history. For the first time I notice a cemetery spread below us. It's unlike any cemetery I know. There are rows and rows of stone boxes standing on the sand. Each stone box is littered with smaller stones. Everything is dirty beige. It looks like a good wind scrubbed the whole place down to rock, and then the dirty sand drifted in and coated everything again. Maybe everything in Jerusalem is dirt-colored like this, and it will seem perfectly normal in a day or two. I've heard that Jerusalem is the color of milk and honey, a thousand beautiful hues of gold. But the descriptive word that comes to my mind is much harsher: hardscrabble.

I am personally acquainted with cemeteries, having lived next door to one in rural Illinois. I sometimes chased cattle who knew to hide behind headstones when the fence broke down. At one funeral where I officiated, an elder explained why all the graves face east: the better to greet Jesus when he returns. After that I liked to picture the scene described in 1 Corinthians 15: angels blasting on trumpets, bodies lifting from graves, pink-tinged clouds forming a throne for Jesus, the whole scene shot through with rays of light, anchored to earth by the rich green of grass. Could my imagination set that triumphant scene here just as well? No grass, no cows, no headstones, no flowers — just littered stone boxes. But Jesus is here, too, of course. Even in a Jewish cemetery. Perhaps especially in a Jewish cemetery. These graves face west, not east, I calculate, since they face the Holy City. They would be prime seats for the Second Coming.

Stephen's voice brings me back to the present. He's talking about the cemetery. "You can be buried here today, but it'll cost you $10,000." I don't intend to pay $10,000 for a plot, not today, and not when my time comes. I look again for the sparrows in the olive tree. Birds of the air don't have that kind of money, either.

"Notice the small stones atop the graves. These are tokens of respect placed by visitors, like flowers. A stone is the first fruit of the desert." When I digest this fact, the graves no longer look littered, but ornamented. Once again I've been given eyes to see what is before me.

Someone points out a church with a gleaming golden dome and asks whether we'll visit it. "The Church of Mary Magdalene, Russian Orthodox," Stephen says. "It was built in 1888. Quite recent, really." Back in the United States, the brick sanctuary in which I preach is 160 years old, and we fall all over ourselves calling it historic. To me it seems ancient. The furnace is ancient, anyway, and the roof —

Four o'clock. A Muslim call to prayer peals from the minarets. The recorded sound is insistent, piercing the Holy City.

CHAPTER 4

Six Degrees

They confessed that they were strangers and foreigners on the earth,
for people who speak in this way make it clear that they are seeking
a homeland.

HEBREWS 11:13-14

B ACK AT THE college, people head to their rooms for a rest.
Mentally exhausted but physically restless, I wander into the
small garden on the grounds. I recognize the head housekeeper,
Khalil, a man in his fifties, and introduce myself and shake his
hand.

"Are there any olive trees around here?" I ask.

Khalil stifles a smile. "No. But do you like fig trees?" He walks
me through a maze of pathways. There are three different species
of fig trees in the garden, and he insists on locating them all.

"What are those?" I point to a fist-sized fruit hanging from
a branch.

Khalil plucks the yellow globe and hands it to me. "Pomegranate."

Of course! I want to say that I would have recognized the fruit
better in its natural environment — grocery store bins — but
doubt the joke would translate. I turn the pomegranate in my
hands, realizing that I've only consumed this fruit as juice. How
do I open it? It's one more thing I don't know about this land.
Not-knowing is what makes me a pilgrim. No, that's not right.
Admitting that I'm not-knowing is what makes me a pilgrim.

Khalil gestures for me to follow him. We tuck around the side of the dormitory and he holds aside a low-hanging branch to allow me to pass. Underneath a canopy of trees are two kitchen chairs with ripped vinyl seats. Between them is a rickety table holding a full ashtray. He offers me a seat, which I accept, and a cigarette, which I decline. I roll the smooth pomegranate between my palms. Khalil puts down his cigarette, pulls out a pocketknife, and deftly slices the fruit open. Like a patient uncle, he pantomimes how I should scoop the seeds.

Our cast-off chairs are on the edge of Saint George's property, inside a cast-iron fence. We sit two feet higher than the sidewalk, behind a screen of trees. We can watch passersby, but they aren't likely to notice us.

"Do you live nearby?" I ask.

"My family lives in Bethany. You Christians know it. You know Mary and Martha and Lazarus."

The pomegranate seeds are messy and pungent. Scooping them feels awkward, but I like crushing them between my teeth. "Have you lived there all your life?" I ask.

"For eight generations," he says.

I can't help but stare as Khalil blows a long stream of smoke. I have no idea what it's like to be so connected to a particular place. My family has been in America for a mere three generations, and I could not tell you, without looking it up first, which cities in the Netherlands they originate from. I personally have lived in eight states, at more addresses than I can remember. As the smoke disappears, Khalil speaks into the air. "Bethany means 'house.' My house."

Armed men appear on the sidewalk below us. I let the tart seeds mash between my teeth. The silence stretches. I reach for a standard getting-acquainted question from my part of the world: "Is Bethany to Jerusalem a long commute?"

"Commute?"

"A distance to travel to work every day."

Khalil closes his eyes. "My family lives in Bethany. But I don't always go home."

"Why?" I ask, knowing it sounds naïve.

His eyes close again, as if to shut out the question. "Because of the Wall."

My knowledge of Middle East politics had been embarrassingly sketchy before this pilgrimage, so I had done some reading to catch up. I read about 1948 and the U.N. Resolution that made Israel a sovereign nation; about the Six-Day War in 1967, which changed boundaries; about the Oslo Peace process; and the Camp David Accords. I read about the wall that Israel is building around the Occupied Territories. Now I worry about how to phrase a question. Finally I just ask, "Isn't there a place to get through?"

Khalil talks rapidly now — about checkpoints and work permits and how they expire and how he has to go around. I'm confused. He has a good job, and what does "go around" mean? But he is talking about a different subject now — about the wedding they're planning for his daughter next year. His smile is big and open. It will be a three-day celebration, and all of Bethany will come.

"You and your family are invited, too," he says, expansively.

I imagine the scene, the flute music, the tables of food, skirts lifting as women dance.

Khalil interrupts my daydream with a question. "Why did you come to Jerusalem?"

"I've always wanted to come here," I say, although it isn't exactly true. I used to be scared of coming here, of the heat and dust and threat of violence. I amend my answer: "I had the opportunity to come, and I didn't want to miss it."

"You flew here on a plane?" I nod.

"Without your husband?" I nod again.

"But you have a husband." He barely waits for the nod before he continues. "Then why did he not come with you?"

"Because of his job. He's a teacher. September is busy. And it costs a lot to travel. This opportunity was just for me, because I'm a minister."

"You are a minister? A religious leader?"

"Yes," I say.

"You lead the prayers?"

An old, feminist instinct flares up inside me. "I lead the prayers. I preach from the Bible. I visit people in the hospital. Everything."

"And your husband permits this?"

I try to tamp down my anger. We come from different worlds. How could I describe mine to him? Can I tell him how I've been wounded because I'm a woman, and how those wounds can still ache? How in the conservative church where I grew up, women were not allowed to be ordained to the ministry, and the denomination fought over "the woman problem"? How the life I live now was unimaginable to my childhood self? How I had to leave behind and start again, which wasn't easy? How I had to shake off certain beliefs and expectations and adopt others? I can barely explain that journey to my relatives. How can I explain it to a Muslim man whose family has been in Bethany for eight generations?

"My husband understands," I say.

Khalil seems to relax. He asks, "Do you have children?"

"Two daughters." I feel absurdly proud as I say it, feeling the urge to add that they're beautiful (as if that is the most important adjective!).

"Who's taking care of them?"

"Well, one's in college, and the other one is home with her dad."

"Her dad?" Khalil sounds puzzled.

"Her father."

"Don't you have a mother? Or sisters? Why is the father caring for children?" His words hang in the air like judgment.

"My sisters live far away," I say. It's easier than explaining that my husband is fully capable of caring for our daughter.

"And your mother — she is old?"

I take the easy way out and nod in agreement, silently begging forgiveness from my mother, who is a young seventy-seven.

Khalil exhales a few long smoke rings. "Do you fly away in an airplane by yourself very often?"

"Not as often as I'd like," I say.

He tries to cover the fact, but he is aghast. He gestures toward my pomegranate as he lights another cigarette. "Is it good?"

"It is." I offer him the fruit. He waves it away.

"I have a brother living in Alexandria, Virginia, who works as a limo driver. He is always telling me to come to visit."

"Alexandria is only twenty or twenty-five miles from where I live," I tell him. "You could come and see all the sights of Washington, D.C."

"Abraham Lincoln," he says.

"Lincoln was a great man. His memorial is the best."

"Maybe I visit my brother and see this," he says. "Someday."

Six degrees of separation, it is said, between every pair of humans on the planet. How many ways are Khalil and I connected? Maybe one of those connecting threads is an American hero wearing a stovepipe hat.

Some of the other workers come out for a smoke break, laughing and talking rapidly in Arabic. They freeze when they see me.

"Thanks for the pomegranate, Khalil." I stand up and acknowledge the other workers as I return to my room.

🌱 🌱 🌱

Dinner is chicken and saffron rice in the crowded dining room. I sit with JoAnne and Kyle as they talk Anglican politics — bishops and appointments — things that Presbyterians ignore. I tune out their conversation and plan what I'll say at my rooftop interview. I want to talk about the olive tree and the sparrows, but I'm afraid all my inchoate thoughts will be reduced to a sentimental sound bite: *I walked today where Jesus walked.* As Kyle dissects the implications of a certain bishop's appointment, I silently rehearse: *The Spirit came alive for me under an olive tree as I watched sparrows fly through the branches.* That might work, especially if I quote the Scripture that came into my mind. But I don't want to sound prosaic, or "bedside devotional." The problem is that sound bites sound like sound bites.

No, the real problem is that I'm not ready to articulate these thoughts. If this were a sermon in progress, I'd shelve it for a while and keep on reading and thinking, until the ideas could get some words on their bones, until the Spirit could do its work. What else, what more could I share about today? A Muslim man plucked a pomegranate for me and I glimpsed the sad face of Jesus? True, but did Khalil's face remind me of Jesus simply because it was Middle Eastern and lined with suffering? Or was it that he, a stranger, fed me? I think of Mary Magdalene running into the risen Jesus outside the tomb and mistaking him for the gardener (John 20:14-16).

Stephen's comment — pilgrimage is like a well — seems right, and we're here to look for Jesus everywhere, to search for that refracted glimpse of Love. Did I catch that likeness in my conversation with Khalil? We tried to enter each other's worlds. We didn't do it perfectly, but we made the effort. So, yes, in that sense, Jesus was present.

For some people, my comment about seeing Jesus in the face of a Muslim man might seem like heresy. To others it might seem inconsequential, even boring. All roads lead to the mountaintop, they'll say with a shrug. But where I come from there's only one road, and nobody, especially a religious leader, should go around mixing Muslims with Jesus.

An employee checks the food dishes on the buffet and sneaks a glance at me. He was one of the men surprised to see me talking to Khalil. JoAnne and Kyle are still talking church politics, and I use my knife to saw vigorously on a piece of chicken. I didn't come to Jerusalem to rip apart my belief system. I came to follow the Spirit, to encounter Jesus in his land, amid his stories. I'm beginning to realize that I may have a pocket-sized version of Jesus, and being in Israel is enlarging that. Perhaps, at long last, I'm growing up.

As I tear a round of pita bread in half, I consider questions about Muslims and Jesus that I've suppressed over the years. There's the story of Isaac and Ishmael, the two sons of Abraham by different mothers. I was taught that God didn't intend the rivalry between those brothers, that it began because of sin, specifically Sarah's lack of faith in God's promise that she'd have children as numerous as the stars. Sarah, who was beyond childbearing age, with the years clicking along, helped God out by sending her handmaiden, Hagar, to get pregnant by Abraham. That child was Ishmael. A few years later Sarah gave birth to Isaac. In a fit of jealousy, Sarah banished Hagar and Ishmael to the desert, and they survived only because God intervened.* From Ishmael came the Muslims; from Isaac came the Jews.

It strikes me now that it's unfair, in this pivotal story, to fault Sarah for trying to help Yahweh make good on a most unlikely promise. You could even call Sarah's actions a form of creative faithfulness. Besides, if God created humans, didn't God know that Sarah would do what she did? In fact, didn't God set her up to do exactly that? Making that far-fetched promise and then making her wait so long for its fulfillment? Was God toying with her?

God chose Abraham to covenant with, but the blessing of that reached further, to "all the families of the earth" (Genesis 12:2-3). This text must mean something more than what I've been taught. What if I took it at face value? One was chosen, but for the sake of all. Why have Christians felt entitled to claim this promise of chosenness, anyway? Maybe we're already riding in on the "all the families" phrase. Maybe that phrase can include Muslims, the other children of Abraham.

I inhale the scent of the yellow rice on my plate. This sweet, slightly metallic scent of saffron must be the smell of religion, of history, of Scripture. I'm breathing them in together. I've been in this Holy Land for less than twenty-four hours, and already my thinking is under revision. Not that I have any clarity. There are too many impressions in my mind, too much jumble. I can't follow any single thought to where it leads. Instead, I feel like I'm running into walls, which are probably the limits of words, or my upbringing, or my belief system. Perhaps even the limits of my mind.

---

*Read the whole story in chapters 16 and 21 of Genesis.

I pick up my dessert, a ripe plum, and sink my teeth right down to the stone.

🐦 🐦 🐦

At my interview I do what seems safest. I share facts. For instance, I've always thought of Jerusalem as a shining city on a hill, and that isn't accurate. Maybe John Winthrop's figure of speech, so famously echoed by Ronald Reagan, distorted my imagination. Jerusalem is actually built in the confluence of three valleys and is more properly a city nestled between hills. I talk about that in the interview and probably don't sound very eloquent. I didn't write it out because I was worried I would somehow bash Reagan and that would end up in the documentary. Don't documentarians edit films to include the most embarrassing bits? I also talk about the *tsia*/Zion connection because the subject of water feels safe. I don't mention the sparrows because I'm afraid I'll sound, well, flighty.

Afterward, JoAnne and I rehash our interviews. She didn't know what to say, and she found the camera terrifying. This soothes me greatly, especially since she seems so self-assured.

"Oh, and I found out what 'Tabgha' means," she says. "It's the name of the place where Jesus multiplied the loaves and fishes."

I lie down for a moment and, as soon as I shut my eyes, bread multiplies in front of me — Wonder Bread–like slices with golden crusts and billowy white insides. Before I can marvel enough at this miracle, JoAnne is shaking me awake. Time for an evening lecture: "The Israeli/Palestinian Conflict."

I detour to the basement dining room and stir up a cup of Nescafé using double the suggested amount of crystals, and I chug it. Then I run up the two flights of stairs to the conference room to get my blood pumping. It works. I open my notebook, ready to record the chronology of religious hatred.

....

CHAPTER 5

Opposing Forces

*From one ancestor [God] made all nations to inhabit the whole
earth . . . so that they would search for God and perhaps grope for
him and find him — though indeed he is not far from each one of us.*

ACTS 17:26-27

M ORNING COMES TOO soon. Today is the first day we
must wear "modest" clothes because we'll be visiting
holy sites. We need to cover our knees and shoulders. I put on a
short-sleeved T-shirt and long pants, then tie a silk scarf around
my waist in case I need to cover my head. JoAnne is puttering
around, and I'm in a hurry to get some coffee, hoping it'll chase
away the vestiges of last night's demons.

In the dining room I fix a cup of double-strength Nescafé, then
help myself to a soft, warm pita and a hard-boiled egg. I carry it to the
table where three of the men — Lutheran Michael, Baptist Charlie,
and Anglican Kyle — are deep in conversation. Michael and Charlie
are roommates, getting along famously. Kyle, the Anglican priest
on sabbatical, is spending all his time with the documentary group.

"We were just talking about the Gospel of Mark," Kyle says.
"I read it last night and counted that Jesus crosses the Sea of
Galilee six times."

As I slice my hard-boiled egg over the pita in overlapping
circles, part of my brain wonders how Kyle had the time and energy to read an entire Gospel yesterday. It's taking all my energy
to manage the emotions stirred by this pilgrimage.

"Do you know why he crosses that often?" Kyle asks, then answers his own question. "The devout Jews are on the west side of the lake, and the Gentiles are on the east side, so just by his movements, we can see Jesus trying to unite the two sides."

"Or maybe he just didn't have a map," says Michael, clearly gratified when Charlie laughs.

"So you don't think there's anything more to it?" Kyle is leaning forward. "You don't think the writer of Mark's Gospel was trying to communicate anything through his structure?"

"Why do you people always make it so hard?" Charlie shakes his head. "Why not let the Bible just say what it says?"

🌱   🌱   🌱

After breakfast our group of forty is divided into smaller groups, each of which will explore a specific quarter of the Old City of Jerusalem. "Quarter" doesn't mean fourth, though there are four of them. "Quarter" means living quarter: Muslim Quarter, Christian Quarter, Armenian Quarter, Jewish Quarter. Our documentary group is broken in half, each with a cameraman. Brian, Jessica, Shane, and I are assigned to the Muslim Quarter.

The Old City is just down the road from Saint George's campus. We enter through the Damascus Gate, which looks exactly like the entrance to a castle, with enormous wooden doors flung open. There are only a few people coming and going this early on a Saturday morning. Inside the gate, the streets are really alleyways, with walls close on both sides, and stone underfoot, uneven enough to make my sandals wobble. Everything — walls, pavement, windowsills — is made of stone the color of a dirty yellow dog. The light isn't strong, not this early anyway, with high walls on either side. Garbage is piled in every corner, stinking like rotten fruit. Cats prowl around the edges, most of them mangy. Cooking odors drift into the street.

The Muslim Quarter feels like poverty.

We walk without direction, and the heat rises as we go. The camera follows us, sneaks up on us, zooms ahead to catch us from the front. I am hot, and the strap of my bag, heavy with two water bottles, tugs on my sweating shoulder.

We wander until we stumble across the Monastery of the Flagellation. The name makes me wince, even though we can see a lovely garden with blooming plants. We go through a gate into a courtyard. A plaque says that this is the first stop on the Via Dolorosa. A man approaches us, saying hello in different languages in rapid sequence. He is young and fit, with short, dark hair, dressed in a close-fitting T-shirt and jeans, a thick chain swinging from his back pocket. His English sounds British, which may explain the punk look.

"My name is Michael," he says. "I can be your guide for the day."

"Is your name really Michael?" Brian asks.

"I say 'Michael' to the tourists." He lights a cigarette. "I'm Tercier."

"Where are you from, Tercier?" asks Jessica. She has the most engaging way of addressing people, that genteel Southern quality.

"I was born in Bethlehem to Muslim parents." He drops the sentence like a stone in water and turns his head away as if he doesn't care how it ripples. I wonder how many times a day he says this to Christian pilgrims.

"You were raised Muslim?" Jessica asks. "What do you believe now?"

I wonder if Jessica always goes straight to the religious point, or if this is the effect of last night's lecture. Maybe it's just the air in this Holy Land.

Tercier spits out his reply: "I am an atheist! I believe in nothing!" The group takes a collective step backward at his intensity. "How can I believe in God when I live here? Religion is good for nothing but hatred." He drags deeply on his cigarette. His expression changes, softens. "Tell me. Do you believe in Jesus?"

"Yes," Jessica says, and the rest of us nod and murmur.

"Then why hasn't he come back?" Tercier shifts back on his boot heel, raises an eyebrow.

"It isn't time," Jessica says evenly. "He'll come when it's time."

Tercier is not impressed. "Here is a joke told me by my grandmother: 'Why hasn't Jesus come back?'" He pauses and stabs the air with his cigarette. "'He has. He's in the West Bank and can't get a permit.'" He laughs mirthlessly at this punch line.

Before we walk away, Jessica thanks Tercier for his time. Shane mutters under his breath. I myself cannot condemn the man's atheism. It's more logical than belief, especially in this place that has been decimated by belief. Belief has a shadow side. That shadow grows out-sized in some places. For the first time, it occurs to me that my belief in God is perhaps an indulgence, something I'm free to allow myself because of my sheltered circumstances. I want to go back to Tercier and ask him something, even though I don't know what. I finish off my first water bottle as I try to frame the question. I'm still thirsty.

We continue on, stopping at a tiny shop so Shane can buy some groceries. He doesn't like the food served at the college and wants to buy peanut butter and crackers. From the conversation I realize that he has eaten almost nothing since we got here.

The shop is crammed with merchandise. Bins hold packaged groceries or small toys. Buckets contain loose herbs. Carved wooden statues line one wall, and cheap necklaces hang from a display. A rack of colorful fabric catches my eye. On one side hang bras and panties, on the other side headscarves. Do Muslim women come in to purchase undergarments, then choose a matching *hijab*? The male shopkeeper, dressed in a linen robe and red-checked headscarf, notices me eyeing the underwear. He pulls down a fuchsia bra and thrusts it at me, leering. I pretend that I don't understand his intention.

Fortunately, Shane has found the peanut butter and is asking about crackers. The shopkeeper speaks good English. When he finds out that we're all Christian ministers, he tells us he is Muslim. He says, "We all worship the same God. We are all brothers and sisters." He speaks about the floods in the United States, referring to the big hurricane, Katrina, which must have affected some of his distant family members. He doesn't use the word "refugee," yet conveys that notion. He has sympathy, yes. "Flood is God's judgment," he says with great conviction.

"What do you mean by that?" Brian asks. John moves in closer, video camera on shoulder. The shopkeeper notices the camera and says nothing more.

When we leave, I wonder what the shopkeeper will say in Arabic to his friends after the camera is gone. Whether Christian or Muslim, a theology of divine retribution is unacceptable to me. I dig out my second water bottle and drink most of it.

We continue walking aimlessly. The streets have become crowded and the cooking odors intense. Every so often a boy passes, swinging a sort of pendulum plank suspended from three chains. The plank holds small cups of Turkish coffee and a bowl of sugar cubes. The coffee looks black and scalding; I feel like snatching a cup each time one passes. From time to time Brian and John stop and consult their map. We are looking for a certain place, it seems, although I hardly pay attention. I just follow when they move on.

It's well past noon before we stop for lunch. We have wandered through a maze of streets to arrive at an Austrian hospice, a place of hospitality. "The food is good here," John assures us. At this point I would eat anything. I would drink anything.

We go up stone steps into a multistory building. There's a sign pointing to a café, but we turn toward a chapel first. It is small and beautiful, with richly colored paintings all around and ornamentation on every inch. What hidden beauty! I can only kneel at the prayer rail and feast my eyes. I bypass the painted crowds of saints with their halos and go straight to the Latin words that arc over their heads. Syllable by syllable, I parse: *All people everywhere praise God. All people in heaven everywhere praise.*

To my own astonishment, I start weeping. I'm grateful that John turns off the camera, and when he does, I weep harder. I'm tired and thirsty and feeling both the pain and the beauty of this place. The faces of the atheist Tercier and the Muslim shopkeeper are clearer before me than these beautifully painted saints. How crazy this place is, how perverted by religion! Yet we are commanded: All people everywhere praise God.

I do. I praise God. But how can all people everywhere praise God when we cannot agree on who God is? What if one person's notion of God is so offensive that it keeps another person from believing? What we are clearly commanded to do seems impossible. Impossible. In my mind I have come to the end of what is possible. And I have been in Jerusalem only a few hours. Some pilgrim I am.

When I finish crying, I'm alone. I find a restroom. It has luxurious cool-water taps, and I wash my face, which is blotchy from heat and tears. To think I put on makeup this morning and worried about looking good for the camera. I find my way to the café, where the group has ordered lunch. I pull out a chair and listen to Shane and Jessica discuss doctrine. I try to understand what their differences are and why they matter, but can't. The waiter brings the first course: a little plate of hummus, a basket of pita, a small bowl of diced cucumbers and tomatoes. I scoop up hummus and listen to Jessica and Shane with one ear.

John turns on the camera to catch the conversation, so I move to stay out of the picture frame. Shouts drift in from the street. The smell of hot oil mixes with the pungency of saffron. At the next table a group of tourists sits down with mugs of beer. I lick my lips and look away from their sweating glasses. I can't suggest drinking beer in the middle of the day, can I? What would Jessica and Shane think? Although, really, it's past two o'clock. I'd love to take the edge off. There is too much passion in this place.

We don't last long after lunch. To leave the Old City, we must pass again through the Damascus Gate. Foot traffic has increased greatly. What was a lazy passageway this morning is now like the D.C. Beltway with more people coming in than going out. Worse, there are no lanes, no vehicles, no rules. Just bodies. The throng squeezes like two opposing ropes running both ways through a pulley. I see John hold the camera high over his head, pointed down at the mass of people. I want to see that footage because I can hardly believe what we are about to do.

I deliberately wedge myself between two people heading out. It works. I get carried away, literally — my feet inches off the ground. A person going in the opposite direction gets wedged against my other side, pushing against my pull. Picture it. The full length of my body is pressed against three strangers, each speaking a language I can't comprehend and going a different direction. Is this an ecstasy of oneness with the universe, or a terrifying intrusion into my personal space?

On the other side of the gate I feel like a collie who needs to shake her coat. We regroup and make sure we still have our bags. *Poor crackers,* I think, seeing Shane's smashed backpack. We walk back to Saint George's College, up Salahadeen Street, which pulses with vehicles.

We pass flocks of girls who appear to be in school uniform on this Saturday: navy V-neck jumpers with dropped waists and pleated skirts, worn over pink shirts and long pants, closed shoes. Each head is covered with a white or pink headscarf. So many clothes in such heat! The girls hold hands or link arms, three or four abreast. They speak to each other with lowered heads and giggles. Groups of young men stand around, watching them pass.

A woman in Western dress brushes past me, her cell phone ringing. Among other words, I hear "Mama" in an inflection that is irritated, affectionate, and pleading, all at the same time. I can't decipher what language she's speaking, but I know I've overheard the universal conversation between mother and daughter. My own two daughters seem far away, and I miss them with a physical pain in my chest. For the remainder of the walk I pray fervently for their well-being, and for my husband. I am not only a pilgrim; I am a mother and a wife.

☙ ☙ ☙

In the late afternoon, all the small groups return to the lecture hall to report on their adventures. The stories range widely. After dinner the whole group has a vespers service. Ashley leads, exuding energy in an unexpected way. The group is middle-aged to elderly, and it's the end of a long day; yet Ashley leads with zest and elicits responses: God is great! All the time!

Later, as we're getting ready for bed, JoAnne comments that the service seemed charismatic and asks if that's typical of Presbyterians.

"What do you mean, 'charismatic'?" To me that word implies gifts of the Spirit and speaking in tongues.

JoAnne thinks for a moment. "It demanded something I was unwilling to give."

I think of how often that has happened already on this pilgrimage.

CHAPTER 6

Compelled

As a captive to the Spirit, I am on my way to Jerusalem, not know-ing what will happen to me there.

ACTS 20:22

O N SUNDAY MORNING our documentary group attends wor-ship at Saint George's Cathedral, which is located beside our dorm. The congregation of some thirty-five souls is spread over the large space. They are mainly older women, and are very welcoming. The cathedral isn't terribly grand, as cathedrals go. But it is made of stone, with arched pillars separating the side aisles, and hung all around with colorful banners.

The sermon, "Dimensions of Love," is on Ephesians 3:16-21, the passage that says we are rooted and grounded in love. The bulletin is in English, but when the minister preaches, he does so in Arabic. I put my journal away, since I can't take notes. After ten minutes or so, I sit up straight at the sound of English. He has begun again, preaching in English this time. I pull out my journal, thinking how hospitable it is for him to do this for us.

The preacher talks of rooting and grounding in terms of four dimensions — height, depth, breadth, and width. These are the dimensions of eternity and also the dimensions of the cross. This makes the sign of the cross the sign of perfection and eternity. I roll that around in my head, trying to hear it as God's word to me today, instead of potential sermon material.

The priest tells a story about a desert monk who was persecuted for making the sign of the cross. When asked to speak at the table before a meal, he cleverly made the sign of the cross by gesturing to various dishes as he praised them. So in his own way, without directly speaking the words of prayer, he blessed the food. The priest ties this story to the incarnation of Jesus Christ. Perhaps there is something of a translation barrier, but I feel like I'm groping around the edges of a new understanding about God's love, which could be enfleshed, literally, in the dishes on the table. Can Christ's presence be covert?

The hymns we sing are familiar: "All Hail the Power of Jesus' Name"; "Psalm 23" (the Scottish version); "Praise to the Lord, the Almighty"; and "Stand Up, Stand Up for Jesus." The military language of the last one, exhorting "ye soldiers of the cross," gives me the kind of schoolgirl giggles that come from extreme discomfort. Why would we sing this song in this land — with its Crusader history?

After church comes rest time, and a few of us take a walk to the newest section of West Jerusalem. It's a largely commercial area built after 1948, when the nation of Israel was established. Office buildings, pedestrian malls, banks. We walk for about an hour and see many ultra-orthodox Jews, wearing black hats and prayer shawls, who never glance at us. We pass The Holy Bagel Bakery many times, until it becomes a reference point. Every time I see it, I'm happy to see it again. I want to stop and buy a holy bagel, but my companions keep walking. They are intent on scouting places for possible nightlife.

We return to the college courtyard just in time to set off again. This time the entire group of forty is going to see the model of the Second Temple, which is housed at the Holy Land Hotel. I realize too late that we'll be in an outdoor courtyard under the blazing sun, and I didn't bring my hat.

We pilgrims strike familiar stand-and-listen poses. Stephen begins his lecture by saying that 70 to 80 percent of Israeli Jews today are secular, meaning that they do not practice their religion. He goes on to talk about the model of the city, leaving my mind where it has run aground. What if he were to say that 70 to 80 percent of Christians are secular? I would not comprehend. No, that's not true. I would comprehend. America is full of people who reduce the power of Christian faith to an obligatory church visit twice a year. Would they be considered secular Christians? But does that describe 70 to 80 percent? That statistic would tear the guts right out of Christianity. That statistic would make me weep with despair — and with a sense of my own inadequacy to respond.

So how is it different for Jews? Is it more acceptable to be secular if you're Jewish rather than Christian? That doesn't track. Are there secular Muslims, too? What does that mean? I thought certain words implied "sacred" — that is, if you combined them with "secular," you would create an oxymoron. Yet Stephen just said that 70 to 80 percent of Israeli Jews are secular. Why aren't we all standing around with our mouths agape?

I've been having a conversation in my head, missing the stream of information. Stephen is gesturing to the model of Jerusalem, which spreads out like a prairie dog village. He points out the places where the city walls have been located during different times in history. The lecture lasts a full hour and a half.

☙ ☙ ☙

After a supper of chicken and yellow rice, it's time for Evensong at the cathedral at Saint George's. Attendance is down to a handful, so few that we sit behind the pulpit in the divided wooden seats usually reserved for the choir. It is uncomfortable but intimate, and the cathedral glows with twilight.

The preacher is Nael, the assistant priest at St. George's, whom our group has been getting to know in courtyard conversations in the evenings. He gives the sermon on Acts 20:22: "And now, compelled by the Spirit, I am going to Jerusalem, not knowing what will happen to me there." What a fitting verse for a pilgrim! Nael's talk makes me feel a kinship with the apostle Paul, even though I'm not always a fan. Paul's writings are the ones most often used to keep women out of leadership roles in church, so he and I have wrestled a few rounds. But here at last is something the apostle and I share. We both felt compelled to go to Jerusalem, not knowing what would happen to us there.

Nael talks about the two-thousand-year witness of Palestinian Christians and how it's changing. Christians are leaving, diminishing the worshiping communities. Someday Jerusalem may become a sort of spiritual Disneyland rather than a place of vibrant Christian faith. Nael urges us to look for the face of Christ in every person we meet. We don't know when we will encounter Christ. "Especially in this Holy Land," he says. "Christ could be anywhere."

After church, people gather for a glass of wine in the courtyard. What a delightful change from the coffee and cookies offered at my own church after worship. We chat with some of the people staying in other quarters at Saint George's. I meet Paul, a young priest from the United States, interning at Saint George's for one year. I also meet an older man who tells me he's a scientist who was imprisoned by the Israeli government for whistle-blowing related to nuclear weapons. He's gregarious and very comfortable telling his story. The two women across from him are from Sweden, here on the "Ecumenical Accompaniment Program" of the World Council of Churches, and they've just spent a few weeks in one of the Palestinian refugee camps. They're eager to speak to this local celebrity.

Charlie sits down to talk to Paul about his job at Saint George's, which is essentially Paul's seminary fieldwork, similar to what Charlie is doing in his Baptist church in South Carolina. After they compare notes about their duties, Charlie asks Paul, "What's it like to minister in the Holy Land? Isn't the devil really powerful?"

"Isn't he powerful everywhere?" answers Paul.

"No doubt," says Charlie. "But here worst of all."

Kyle joins the conversation, with a number of issues on the tip of his tongue. I feel a trifle irritated because I wanted to see where the devil talk would go.

Kyle says to Paul, "I'm curious about whether you use the Nicene Creed in your work here."

"To some extent," Paul reponds.

"Baptists don't do creeds," Charlie says.

"More's the pity," Kyle says. "The Nicene is such a foundational creed. People think it's unifying, but it's actually quite divisive."

"How do you mean?" asks Charlie. I notice that he is always willing to listen to Kyle.

"It was written in 381 to read 'the Spirit proceeds from the Father.' But in about 1000, the West added 'and the Son,' which pretty much destroys any chance at ecumenical dialogue. Do you see? So Paul, here you are in the middle of all these faiths, and I want to know: What's your opinion?"

Before Paul can answer, he's called away.

"This is exactly why we don't do creeds," Charlie says. "They're nothing but trouble."

For once I can understand Charlie's perspective, even though I'm a word person and the Reformed tradition is full of creeds. Words can be a tool or a weapon, even when they're ancient. They're never really dead. A few words have the power to enliven or to enrage, the power to build a bridge or to fortify a wall.

☙ ☙ ☙

Back in our simple dorm room, JoAnne shuts the window so that the Muslim midnight call to prayer won't wake us up, as it did the previous night. There's a minaret just outside. Even though the room is a little too warm with the window closed, I agree. Tonight I want to sleep more than I want to pray.

....

CHAPTER 7

Sin-cere

Lord, my heart is not proud.

PSALM 131:1 (NIV)

O N THE BUS waiting to go to the Wailing Wall, I realize that yesterday was September 11, the anniversary of the terrorist attacks on the Twin Towers and the Pentagon. At home in Washington, D.C., that date would have been significant; here it slipped past me. I feel disconnected from my normal life. Maybe my transformation into a pilgrim has been too successful.

It's perplexing, because in other ways I feel like a pilgrim failure. I have good intentions. I want to open myself like a pilgrim. I pray to become whatever God wills. But I get in my own way. Instead of confronting the Holy, I confront myself. I have so many limits, from physical to intellectual. Being in the sun exhausts me. I need caffeine. I need a nap. I need time alone. I'm unable to think past certain thoughts. Maybe that's always been the case, only now I'm aware of the logjam. I can feel the pilgrimage pulling me to jump over this pile-up to somewhere new. But to where? It's threatening to think something new. I've known Jesus every day of my life, to my great comfort. Do I dare change that?

Sitting on the bus, I want to sigh and sigh and sigh — as if to expel these tumbling thoughts and so rid myself of discomfort.

Yet I know I'll breathe in something else, something threatening, or wonderful, or both at the same time. What's more, I can't avoid it: I must take in a next breath. Can I trust the Spirit to be in that breath, too?

In last night's sermon, Nael talked about looking for the face of Christ in each person. I take his words seriously because he lives as a Palestinian Christian in a city literally divided by religion. If he can discover Christ in the faces of Muslims and Jews and atheists, maybe I can, too. Even as I'm pondering this, another interpretation occurs to me, a kind of flip side. Perhaps my face can reflect Christ. Perhaps mine can be the face of Christ.

I'm getting a sense — almost a physical sense — of inner divinity unlike anything I've ever felt before. In what way can I house Christ? I've experienced, in lovemaking, a sense of bodily holiness, but this is different. It's not relational, it's more integral to my own self, my own body-occupying self. Simply writing these thoughts in my journal feels threatening. My Calvinist background has taught me I'm unworthy. The phrase "inner divinity" seems heretical. But I let it stand.

Religion is bound up with bodies. That's not a new concept to me, but I'm seeing new implications. Aren't bodies how religion becomes violent? Violence may begin as an emotion, but it's expressed through bodies. Not only through breath and words, but blows! And isn't love the same — beginning in emotion, expressed through bodies. Yes, both sides of spiritual passion — violence and love — are bound up in our very human flesh. Is this a fuller meaning of incarnation than what I've yet grasped?

I feel a new appreciation gestating in me. I'm experiencing, rather than simply understanding, the essential unity of the spiritual and physical realities. We are not just souls housed in bodies. All of creation truly is shot through with the presence of God. Yet I was taught that this truth borders on heresy. No wonder we Calvinists walk through life blind to the Spirit that lurks everywhere.

The bus pulls up to the Dumb Gate. As we unload, I say to

JoAnne, "I'm struck dumb. What a perfect name! Do you know why it's called the Dumb Gate?"

"Not 'Dumb,'" she replies. "'Dung.' As in poop."

"Poop?" I repeat.

Kyle laughs. "All those animals — remember? For Temple sacrifice. This gate leads to the town dump."

"Oh," JoAnne says, like she's just putting things together. "Gehenna."

"Right you are," says Kyle. "Oh hell."

I don't say anything. I'm busy thinking how truly dumb I've been. For all my years of Bible studies, it has never occurred to me just how much dung the Temple would have had to deal with. Funny. The whole point of sacrifice is to make one clean. Yet the process is anything but sanitary.

❦ ❦ ❦

At the Temple Mount we pass through our first security checkpoint. Men and women must separate into two lines. Unsmiling guards with automatic weapons examine our passports, then gesture for our water bottles. As we go through a metal detector, each water bottle receives the same treatment: cap unscrewed, contents sniffed, cap replaced. The contrast between the unused deterrent slung over the shoulder — a high-powered rifle — and the deterrent actually used — a human nose — strikes me. Incarnation yet again. Despite all the technology of violence, security comes down to olfactory glands. On the other side of the checkpoint we women and men rejoin the same stream. I wonder why the nose brigade is concerned with gender, though certainly gender matters everywhere in this Holy Land.

We ascend a long, covered ramp to a plaza which is surprisingly quiet, park-like. Two men in blue uniforms collect garbage with a rolling cart as they chat. Hearing an occasional belly laugh, I suspect that they're comparing weekend stories on this Monday morning.

Our group leader, Stephen, explains why this site is significant to both Jews and Muslims. To the Jews, the Temple Mount is their holiest site, the location of Solomon's Temple, which was destroyed by the Babylonians in 586 BCE and later rebuilt by Herod. Because the exact whereabouts of the Holy of Holies is unknown, many Jews feel they shouldn't enter the area at all — it is too revered.

To the Muslims, the Temple Mount is the third holiest site, where Muhammad ascended to heaven. Islam's two more sacred sites also concern Muhammad: the most sacred is Mecca (where he was born), and the next most sacred is Medina (where he died). The Muslims built the Dome of the Rock as a pilgrim shrine in 691 CE and later built a place of worship, the Al-Aqsa Mosque, which is not as grand and beautiful a building as the Dome.

The rock inside the Dome commemorates another essential story: Abraham binding his son before sacrificing him to God. The story of the binding of Abraham's son is foundational to all three faiths, though there are important differences, such as which son is bound, Isaac or Ishmael, and on which mountain. The profound truth remains the same: Abraham was tested by God. Does it matter where, exactly, the mountain was located? I'm glad that theology trumps geography in this moment.

"You'll find," Stephen says in his understated way, "that in the Holy Land, holy places move."

The Dome before us was gilded in the 1990s, the gold paid for by the King of Jordan. Now the Dome is under the control of Israel. Stephen says that there have been "incidents" here, so security is high. When he puts quotation marks around a word with his voice, Stephen's British accent is particularly pronounced, which sparks my imagination.

"What incidents?" I whisper to the person next to me.

"Someone tried to pour acid on the shrine," the person whispers back. So that explains the olfactory patrol.

Stephen is listing the Five Pillars of Islam, and I jot them down quickly: belief in monotheism/Allah; prayer five times a day; tithing; fasting during the month of Ramadan; pilgrimage to Mecca (hajj) at least once in a lifetime.

As I write, I listen with one ear to the sound of the sprinklers on the lawn. Men hawk postcards as Stephen talks. I'm curious about the lives of ordinary people like the garbage collectors. What is it like to call Jerusalem home?

Stephen points out a mihrab, which points toward Mecca, and I twist myself around, wondering how I would orient my body to point toward Mecca. As happens so frequently on this pilgrimage, I feel like I'm on the threshold of understanding something pivotal. I wish I had just a few minutes to soak it all in. What if I never come back here again? It's hard to know what bits of information matter and what ones don't. Which one will the Spirit use to speak to me? I feel overwhelmed and yet greedy for more.

Stephen is saying something about ablution stations, which are fountains for washing before worship. A supplicant is supposed to wash the whole body, including the mouth, before prayer. And the Muslims say that prayer is better than sleep. As we are herded along, I wonder: *Is prayer better than sleep? I don't live that way. What would happen if I did?*

Stephen points to an area where the Byzantine Christians believed that Jesus cleansed the Temple. I look around the empty plaza and cannot picture it as more than what it is: hot, dry slabs of stone. He gestures to another area of the Temple grounds where the text about Jesus' temptation — the reference to the pinnacle of the Temple — has its own corner. There is no pinnacle to create a picture in my mind, and I'm too busy taking in what's there now to imagine what was there in antiquity.

All around us are huge stone arches with indecipherable engravings. These marks are the scales on which God will measure all humans. Now there's another tidbit that begs for a few moments of reflection. How, exactly, does God measure a human with a stone arch? I stand beneath the arch. I'm five-foot-four-and-a-half. Does the stone measure that? I'm not as kind as I should be. Does the stone measure my failings, too?

We approach the Dome of the Rock itself. "The building is octagonal," Stephen says, "because seven is perfect, but eight is even more perfect."

He doesn't mention the fact that eight is also significant in Christianity. We worship on the eighth day, essentially, because Saturday (the original Sabbath) was the seventh day, but the Sabbath was moved to Sunday in honor of Jesus' resurrection. So the number eight is a number beyond perfection in Christianity, too. Another random fact pops into my head: The early Christians constructed churches in the shape of an octagon if they were sure that Jesus had actually been at that site. Yes, Jesus' presence would perhaps linger, making the place beyond perfection.

I have the sudden urge to turn to someone and suggest that we do a craft project with Popsicle sticks. We could make something eight-sided, something beyond perfection. I need time to digest all this, need to manipulate with my fingers as well as my brain. With a tremendous pang, I wish my daughters were here with me, not as the young women they are now but as the little girls they used to be, when a table set with construction paper, glue bottles, and a shaker of glitter could make them crow with happiness. I need the sweetness of their naïveté because it's the only thing that makes it possible to believe in a notion like "beyond perfection."

The group has moved on and is examining the enormous eight-sided Dome, which is covered with Arabic calligraphy: "There is no God but Allah, and Muhammad is his prophet." Not that I can actually read the inscription. Stephen reminds us that all images are forbidden to Muslims, which is why words and geometric designs ornament the building.

The prohibition against images sounds familiar. "Thou shalt make no graven images" is one of the Ten Commandments (Exodus 20:4-5, KJV). All three of the Abrahamic faiths began with a prohibition against images, yet only Islam has held to it. Why? Are Muslims more obedient to their scripture than Christians are to theirs? The question is like twisting my body around to be oriented by the mihrab toward Mecca. I can't get my mind to follow this thought to its conclusion.

The decorative tiles are blue and green and gold, a mosaic pattern of eight-sided shapes. I wander around the plaza, stopping to put my hand on a marble column. Kyle comes by and asks, "Do you know where the word 'sincere' comes from?" I shake my head and wait while Kyle, a true preacher, pauses for a beat. "From the Latin *sin-cere*, which literally means 'without wax.' When someone ordered marble work, they would specify 'sin-cere,' because holes can be filled with wax and buffed to look like marble."

I love random facts that make me think differently. My college's motto runs through my memory. It's a quote from John Calvin: Cor meum tibi offero, Domine, prompte et sincere ("Lord, I offer you my heart, promptly and sincerely"). It's an interesting quote because Calvin was an intellectual giant, and yet he loved God with his heart as well as his head. Now I glimpse new depths to this word *sin-cere*. Lord, I offer you my heart now, as it is, without wax to hide its flaws. Without buffing, without artifice, without any polishing at all.

Does God really want my unvarnished heart? I've been polishing for so many years that I'm not even sure what my *sin-cere* heart would look like. Four years in seminary certainly count as an application of paste wax. Two decades in ministry certainly function as buffing. Even this pilgrimage began as a wash-and-wax for my spiritual life.

I wander around all eight sides of the Dome, ending by the ablution stations. Ablution, as I understand it, is an extreme form of cleansing. I appreciate the desire for cleanliness. There's some washerwoman embedded in my DNA. But to be clean enough to approach the presence of a sovereign God? That seems like a useless compulsion. A person can never be that clean — isn't that the whole point of grace? We Calvinists, with our emphasis on depravity and sin, understand this. But even while our doctrine says, "It's all grace," we turn around and work and work to be good enough. I've been taught to try harder, to be cleaner, to become more pure.

I wander past the many ablution stations wondering if my new Latin word *sin-cere* can help me unpack these mixed messages. It's hard to think coherently for this long, in this heat. I've emptied my water bottle and I'm still thirsty. Sincerely thirsty. There are many fountains at each ablution station, all dry. The sight of so many useless spigots intensifies my thirst.

Feral cats wander in the corners of the Temple Mount. They are probably thirsty, too. Children appear from nowhere and approach the video cameras, making faces into the lens. Taking all this in, I notice that Marty — the pilgrim who wondered if the week would fundamentally change her — is wearing a white *hijab*. I ask her about it, and she tells me that she bought it yesterday in the Muslim Quarter. It makes her feel adorned, just as her pulpit vestments do. Like most Episcopalian priests I know, Marty loves her vestments. And I have my black robe and simple stole. Suddenly the situation strikes my funny bone. Marty is an Episcopalian priest draped in a Muslim *hijab*, standing under a bright sun next to a waterless fountain and discussing vestments with me, someone who doesn't wear them. Everything is a jumble in this Holy Land!

I blurt out, "I could kill for a beer!" We both laugh.

....

CHAPTER 8

Sisters

Jesus, Son of David, have mercy on me!

MARK 10:47

"THERE'S ANOTHER SECURITY checkpoint before we can enter the plaza," Stephen says.

"You mean by the Wailing Wall?" someone asks.

"Don't call it that. People gave it that name to belittle the Jews who were mourning the destruction of the Temple. It is the Western Wall, and that is what we should call it. We mustn't insult our Jewish brothers and sisters."

I realize I must bow to this piece of history and change my language, but I feel the loss of poetry. Who would choose "Western Wall" over "Wailing Wall"? I will call it the right thing from now on, even though my heart is resistant.

We are allotted fifteen minutes. The men and women visit separate sections of the wall. The men get three-quarters, and the women get the last little piece, which is much more crowded. Even so, the women's section seems quieter than the men's. No theatrics. No wailing. No drums.

Jessica takes a quick picture of me and JoAnne together in front of the women clustered by the wall. Then, alone, I make my way to the wall itself. Two rows of white vinyl chairs face the stones, most of them occupied by women reading the Torah.

Other women stand. Standing or sitting, they bend forward and bob gently as they speak softly to themselves, so the air is a gentle murmur. There is no empty space at the wall, yet no one is shoving. I smell lavender. A few women stand behind the ones praying, waiting for someone to leave. I get into a similar position. Before I'm quite expecting it, a space opens in front of me.

I am a Christian, a Protestant, unfamiliar with worshiping at a holy rock. I'm not sure how to do this. I hold a slip of paper that my Jewish friend Stephanie has given me to leave at the wall. I slip the paper into a crack, then pray for Stephanie, and for her prayer requests, which I have not read.

What next? I look to the side and see that women have their hands spread against the wall. I put my hands up and make contact with my palms. The stone is cool and rough-textured. My glance falls on my watch. The fifteen minutes are already more than half gone. Quick. I want to be in a more prayerful mood. Without meaning to, I lean my forehead against the cool stone. Without meaning to, I pray: *Lord Jesus Christ, Son of God, have mercy on me, a sinner.* It's an Eastern Orthodox prayer that's been memorized by Christians for centuries. The words are from Mark 10, the story of Blind Bartimaeus, whom Jesus healed. It's called the Jesus Prayer.

Is it proper to pray the Jesus Prayer at the Western Wall? Ignoring that question, my heart repeats the prayer. And again. *Lord Jesus Christ, Son of God, have mercy on me, a sinner.* I realize I'm leaking tears. Yes, I'm a sinner. I need mercy. I desire to offer my heart to the Lord, but it is imperfect. I've patched it with wax, but God can see right through. I offer up my imperfect, patched heart. I trust that I can be redeemed.

The tears do not stop, but my heart ceases to hammer. I feel a flood of forgiveness, a sense of peace. Yes, I am impatient and quick to judge. I pigeonhole other people's beliefs and think mine are better. I get cranky and snappish in the heat. But Jesus sees past these sins. I turn my head and press my right cheek against the wall.

There is movement on my left as a young mother lifts her baby alongside the wall. The baby is maybe seven months old, dressed in a red jumper over an embroidered blouse. The mother spreads the little girl's palms against the stone, then gently turns the head. The baby doesn't protest, just rests her left cheek against the wall as if she's done this before. Beneath a colorful head-wrap her eyes are dark brown and somber. An old soul. She looks at me, unblinking. Our faces are about twelve inches apart. My own eyes are curtained by tears, which I blink away because I want to see the baby clearly. The mother has put her own forehead against the wall on the other side of her child. I wonder who she is praying for. This baby? A husband? Other family members? With my eyes open, I pray with her.

Lord Jesus, heal their wounds and bless them, I pray. It doesn't matter that I can't name their wounds; they undoubtedly have some. It doesn't matter that the mother wouldn't pray to "Lord Jesus"; God undoubtedly loves both her and her child. The baby and I stay locked in each other's gaze, with our heads against the wall for some time while the prayer circles through me.

Finally something shifts, and I notice my watch. I'm late. "Forgive me," I whisper to the baby. My sister. Since I've prayed for her and with her, she has taken up residence in my heart. I peel myself away from the wall. I have to concentrate so that I don't turn my back to the wall as I leave. I watch the mother and baby as I back away, feeling incredibly grateful to be here. Grateful that God is here. Oh, for this feeling in our church pews, this emptying of the self.

I stumble toward the tour group, deaf and dumb. My tears leak while Stephen talks on about the original Temple stones. He points out the famed Robinson's Arch, and I finally raise my eyes to look at the wall from this more distant perspective. The original stones truly are gigantic and clean-edged. Higher up, the "newer" stones sprout trailing vines and grasses; pigeons fly about and perch on tiny ledges between the stones. The sight stokes my tears. The stones were so magnificently created, so precisely hewn, so conscientiously aligned.

Ashley and Jessica notice my tears and move toward me.

Kyle puts an arm around my shoulders. I am grateful that I
don't need to explain my tears because I could not. My fellow
pilgrims comfort me.

The group moves to the Southern Wall, where there are piles
of rubble, colossal rocks which fell during the destruction of the
Temple in 70 CE and have remained untouched. But excavation
has exposed stone-lined holes, *mikvaot,* that were used for ritual
baths for Temple purification. Some of the holes have steps leading down, like whirlpool baths, although they have long been dry.
When we're given a few minutes to explore, I step into one of
the holes and wish it had a little water. I could use a foot-soak, a
few moments to help me digest my new emotional connections
to this Holy Land's walls and stones and rubble.

Ashley sits next to me and says, "I felt absolutely nothing at
the wall, but you were crying."

"Wailing, actually," I answer. "You could say I was convicted
of my sin."

She nods sympathetically. "I know what you mean. Sometimes
I feel that way, too. But today I just felt cold."

JoAnne comes by with sprigs of lavender she plucked from the
ruins. Before we even have time to inhale their scent, someone
hurries us along.

"The Byzantine period," Stephen is saying, and I glance at
someone else's notes to jot down the dates: 324-638. I also record
these details: "Excavations from this era. Christian pilgrimage.
Notable pilgrim Egeria whose journal 381 to 384 details Byzantine
ritual." Stephen reminds us of the Psalms of Ascent, or Pilgrim
Psalms: 120–134. I make a mental note to reread them, maybe
to plan a sermon series on them. And just like that, I've slipped
from my pilgrim self into my cerebral professional self.

Stephen begins another lecture, this one addressing a question: Why doesn't the New Testament mention the destruction
of the Temple in 70 CE? To get at that, he lists the dates when the
Gospels were written: Mark is earliest, written in 65, Matthew
in 75, Luke in —

A bar mitzvah procession interrupts him, although he con-

tinues, unfazed. Men in prayer shawls are blowing the shofar
and beating drums, their fringes swinging. It sounds loud and
festive. It sounds like a party. It sounds like more fun than learn-
ing distant dates. I prowl to the edge of the group and peer at
the parade, but cannot spot the guest of honor. I wonder what
it's like to be a Jewish boy under noisy escort to his bar mitzvah
at the Western Wall.

When the lecture is finally over, we are free to explore the
remains of the Second Temple, the Herodian Temple. There is
a section of original steps, and I sit down on them. The stones
are deeply worn, and the edges are crumbled.

"How many centuries would it take to wear stone like this?"
I ask Kyle, as he takes a seat beside me.

"Many," he says. "Or else the sextons were grossly negligent."

Kyle and his Anglican humor. I lay my palms flat against the
dirty stone. Did Jesus' feet touch these very steps? It's not the
kind of question I would normally ask, yet it seems unavoidable.
A thrill goes through my palms and into my fingertips.

According to Luke 2, the Temple was where Jesus' parents,
Mary and Joseph, encountered Simeon and Anna, who were
the first people to recognize that this infant boy was the Messiah. I've always pictured that story taking place on the Temple
steps. Could this be the exact place where the Messiah was first
recognized? The possibility is humbling. Do I deserve to be here?

I don't recognize the presence of the Messiah now. I don't look
for Christ in the faces around me. I gaze at my fellow pilgrims
and feel raw and weary, and thirstier than ever. I want to feel
the presence of Jesus right now, here, on these very steps. But I
cannot command it. Part of me wishes I could, but part of me
is glad that I cannot.

At that moment Brian decides to film our group descending
the steps together. The cameramen calculate spacing and angles.
It feels staged — because it is: we are going from nowhere to
nowhere for the sake of the video. All the people who are not in
the documentary are asked to stand aside. They do so, but make
wisecracks as we pass by.

Finally, we have filmed enough, learned enough, and prayed enough. We trek a ways to have lunch at a Lutheran hospice: pita and hummus, cucumbers and tomato, rice and some kind of meat stew. How I wish they'd bring a pitcher of beer, to cool my feverish emotions. Instead, we drink many pitchers of water.

After lunch we move to a circle of comfortable chairs. Turkish coffee and cake are available. I take a small ceramic cup filled with hot liquid, heavy with grounds. It is very sweet at the same time that it is bitter. Across from me, Charlie leans back and half-closes his eyes. He looks like a contented cat as he says, "It doesn't get any better than this." His face is pink, whether from sun or emotion or both. My heart softens. Could his be the face of Christ?

While we sip our coffee, our chaplain lectures about living stone. He describes cave theology, which says that two of the three salvific events of Christianity took place in rock caves at night: the Nativity and the Resurrection. The third event took place on a rock: the Crucifixion. He goes on to say that Jerusalem bedrock is necessary, not only in a symbolic way, but also in a physical way, because it supports the weight of so many buildings made of stone. He lists some of the weighty buildings, which are everywhere in Jerusalem. Weight. I remember the atheist Tercier, whom we met yesterday. What weight he must feel all around him — the weight of history! I wish I could talk to Tercier again and ask him about the weight that religion lays on his shoulders. I, too, have felt the weight of religious history, of doctrinal fights. But the people around me are not killing each other. Maybe that is why I can still believe.

The chaplain is done talking. I'm loath to get out of my comfortable chair, but we have one more stop, the Christian site. Then we will have seen "the three major holy sites of the three Abrahamic faiths in one city in one day," just as the itinerary promised. I remember how inspiring that sounded before we embarked.

CHAPTER 9

Stone Cold

Come to him, a living stone . . . let yourselves be built into a spiritual house, to be a holy priesthood.

1 PETER 2:4-5

WE WALK ACROSS Jerusalem to the church constructed over the tomb of Jesus. The church was built in the fourth century by Constantine, the emperor who converted to Christianity and ushered in the age of Christendom. Shortly after his conversion, Constantine sent his devout mother, Helena, to establish shrines at the major holy sites. This spot was one of her big discoveries, the actual bedrock of Golgotha, where Jesus was crucified.

"That Helena," Kyle says. "What a nose for relics."

The Orthodox call it the Church of the Resurrection. The Catholics share the building, but they call it the Church of the Holy Sepulchre. What you choose to call it depends on what you want to emphasize: resurrection or grave. Which name shall I call it? It occurs to me that the Presbyterians would have solved the dilemma by simply assigning it a number: "First Presbyterian Church of Jerusalem."

The story goes that the Christian communities in Jerusalem are unable to trust each other with the keys of their church building, so the keys are held by a Muslim. Imagine all the ways you could preach that: "Way to fail, Christians!" Or, "Christians

united by a Muslim — proof that God is greater than any one
belief system!" Or, "Religion is the worst wedge between brothers. It's pure poison!"

"The devil is never still," says Charlie. "Especially here."

The church is a maze of chapels and levels. We begin upstairs
in a chapel built over the rock where Jesus was crucified. The
room is hushed. There is a chest-high altar made of white marble
that reminds me of a fireplace mantel. At the base of the altar is
a hole, which, we are told, reaches to the bedrock of Golgotha.
We watch people get on their hands and knees and reach, as if
to light a fire in a fireplace. They're putting a hand through the
hole to touch the rock.

We wait our turn. One by one, each pilgrim kneels, crawls a
few steps, reaches his or her hand down, then backs out. Some
people linger; others hurry. Afterward, a few stop to wipe their
eyes, while others look glazed.

When it's my turn, I find it awkward and humbling to go
down on all fours. There's a picture of Jesus at eye level when
you're on your hands and knees. The picture is covered with glass,
and there are smudges where people have kissed or touched the
glass. I have an instant aversion, yet when I see Jesus' face, tears
spring to my eyes and I kiss the glass, too. I must be a pilgrim.
It is quite curious because the picture is nothing special. The
Jesus of that picture looks like a million historically incorrect
Sunday school pictures: his hair too straight and light, his nose
too aquiline, his skin too pale. Intellectually, I reject the likeness;
yet my eyes well up as I study it. Whatever Jesus looked like, this
is where he died.

I don't have time for all these feelings; people are waiting. I
feel like a child in a Touch and See Room, where you lift the flap
and reach in blind, trying to identify shell or wood or antler by
touch, ready to be either delighted or repulsed. I reach my hand
through the hole. The bedrock of Golgotha is both jagged and
polished under my fingertips. Touching it is both comforting and
unsettling. I gasp and withdraw my hand. Backing out of the
fireplace/altar is even more awkward than crawling in.

Perhaps this is what pilgrimage is all about: being invited into the appropriate posture of humility; being invited to confront these essential, complicated feelings; being invited to feel gratitude, even if you can't say precisely what you're grateful for.

I notice that Ashley's face is tear-streaked. As our eyes meet, she says, "He died for me!" and begins to cry again. I put my arm around her shaking shoulders. I know she and I could talk theology all day, parsing that simple sentence. But also at this moment I understand her tears without having to explain them. I, too, have a sense of remorse mixed with gratitude.

As the group slowly regathers, Stephen prepares us for the next stop, downstairs, where there is a place for devotion, a granite slab referred to as the Stone of Anointing. Tradition holds that the body of Jesus was laid here when it was taken from the cross. Stephen says that people pray at the stone, or kiss it, or leave offerings.

The stone is exactly the size you would expect, the size of a man stretched out. Over the slab, eight ornate oil lamps hang on heavy chains. There are people kneeling at the stone. I wait my turn, then kneel and put both hands on the pink-toned marble. I imagine Jesus' body lying on that stone, bloodied and pierced. The stone is cold, and I begin to weep. A deep sense of unworthiness makes me feel hot. I am beginning to tire of feeling unworthy, yet it's my automatic response, a response in both body and mind. I lean forward and lay my forehead on the cool stone. Almost automatically I begin an endless loop of the Jesus Prayer. *Lord Jesus Christ, Son of God, have mercy on me, a sinner.* I want to loop through it until I wear out the words, or at least understand them, but others are waiting. I'm sure that others feel unworthy, too. I will relinquish my spot at the mercy seat.

We descend another flight of stairs and visit another chapel. This one was established by the Armenians, the first people to become officially Christian in 301, pre-Constantine. The Armenians are proud of this heritage. Lower still, in a great cave of bedrock, is a chapel to Saint Helena, Constantine's mother.

In the stone walls leading to these two deepest chapels, the

Crusaders have carved crosses. There are so many crosses you would be hard-pressed to find room to squeeze another one in. There are Crusader crosses all over this church. I had noticed them in the pillars beside the entrance doors when we came in. In fact, those stone pillars are so deeply etched that they appear to be made of wood. As I trace one of the crosses with my fingertips, I imagine the fervent knights leaning on their knife blades. Gouging stone seems like a strange way to express devotion. Are these crosses adornment or defilement? Or an ancient form of graffiti?

The period of the Crusades, a thousand years ago, was a dark one in Christian history. Religious conviction propelled soldiers from Western Europe to push east to the Holy Land, which they wanted to wrest from the infidels, the Muslims. The Crusaders forced their beliefs on both Muslims and Jews by forcibly baptizing them. They killed those who refused. The Crusaders were soldiers of the cross, taking their very name from *crux* (Latin for "cross"). Their purpose was to reclaim Jerusalem, the place where Jesus was crucified, to open it to Christian pilgrims.

I'm sure it pains Jesus to know the bloodshed that was done in his name. As a pilgrim, it pains me to have any part at all in this history. Yet I feel the power of pilgrimage, of people making this journey for the sake of their beliefs. There's an inherent power in a pious purpose. My fingers cannot stay away from one of the crosses etched in stone. I wonder about the Crusader who carved it. What did he believe? What drove him? I feel the primitive beauty of the simple lines. Was it a mammoth effort to carve these lines, or was this Crusader so overcome with religious fervor upon reaching this sacred place that it was a trifling thing for him to press the point of his knife blade into solid stone?

"They're beautiful, aren't they?" Charlie says as I linger over the crosses.

"I can't decide if they are or not," I answer. "Do they defile the wall or adorn it?"

"Blood atonement isn't pretty," Charlie says. "But thank the Lord for it!"

There's no mistaking the piety in my fellow pilgrim's heart. Charlie loves Jesus. He asks me for a page and pen so we can make a rubbing of the cross. The rubbing doesn't come out well without the right tools, but at least it's some kind of evidence of where we've been, a kind of paper trail that we are working out our own salvation by being here, by exploring these ideas (Philippians 2:12). Perhaps the rubbing is an attempt to reconcile the opposing forces of religious history: piety and oppression. Perhaps the rubbing is foolish. Perhaps every pious enterprise appears foolhardy when seen from great time and distance.

In a few moments the whole group stops again, this time at the Chapel of the Prison of Jesus, which honors those who are prisoners of conscience. We crowd into the small space in order to conduct a brief prayer service. My body presses against the warmth of an elderly pilgrim on one side and cold stone walls on the other.

We have been in the church for more than an hour. Stephen says that now we will go to two chapels, each with the "original" tomb. The first chapel is used by the Syrians, though it's owned by the Armenians. The walls are coated black with incense.

"Why don't they clean the walls?" someone asks.

"Because neither side will pay for clean-up or renovation," Stephen answers. "Each thinks the other should pay."

He smiles wryly and we return the smile. We are beginning to understand this Holy Land.

This Syrian/Armenian chapel has a *koch* tomb (from the Hebrew for "oven"). Stephen says that this may not be the original tomb, but it's a terrific model for how the real tomb probably looked. I look around and don't believe him. He can't know everything. Someone gave him bad information. This is certainly not the way the tomb of Jesus looked in my Sunday school lessons. Everyone can picture the rock that was rolled before that tomb — a nice, round rock, clean and white. After all, it was a perch for angels!

But we are deep underground. There's not a bit of natural light. Nothing is white or clean. Picture a black wall with a brick oven set into it, the kind for making pizza. That oven door opens into the tomb. Each tomb has two parts. In the larger front part, the "foyer," so to speak, the body would be anointed. Then the body would be pushed into the second part, one of the deeper recesses, and the tomb would be sealed. Eighteen months later a family member would open the tomb and scrape the bones together and put them in an ossuary, or bone box. In the Hebrew scriptures this scraping/gathering is what is meant by the phrase "and he was gathered to his fathers." Stephen makes scraping motions with his arms to cement our understanding. I shiver involuntarily.

We are allowed to enter the tomb three at a time. Kyle, myself, and a woman from another pilgrim group stoop very low to enter. We are practically on our knees on a filthy floor. We shine the flashlight around. The only other light comes from a single wick burning in an oil candle. There are multiple doors all the same size: small. You couldn't crawl into those doors. We are in the shared foyer, and the doors lead to the deeper recesses. You'd have to lie down and have someone shove you in. Head-first or feet-first? We count two open doors and two sealed doors.

"Are there bodies in there?" the woman asks.

"Yes," Kyle says confidently, as if he knows.

We all shudder. Then we crawl back out. We cross a large, open area to another chapel to see a second original tomb. This one is housed in a structure made of stone and marble that is ornately carved. This tomb is closely supervised. A man who is distinctively dressed in a round fur hat and long black robe lets people into the tomb four at a time. He signals entrance and exit every few minutes by clapping his hands vigorously, which makes his enormous cross necklace swing against his chest. We wait obediently until he claps for us.

Inside the structure, the tomb itself is all marble. At least it feels clean. The washerwoman part of my DNA is happy. I put my shekel in the box to pay for a candle. When I kneel to light the candle, I am beside Michael, and our knees are on the marble floor. Ashley and Jessica are on Michael's other side. I feel depleted rather than Spirit-filled. Maybe I've used up my

*I feel like this
Spirit me*

allotment of Spirit for the day. Maybe the Spirit can't penetrate all the marble. Maybe the fur-hatted man clapping his hands drives the Spirit away.

When we leave, I'm glad that this is the last site on the agenda.

❦   ❦   ❦

We find the other members of the documentary group to discuss logistics. Then we all walk slowly back through the Old City of Jerusalem toward the Damascus Gate, shopping as we go. When some of the others buy small silver Jerusalem crosses on necklace chains, I decide this is a good idea. I try to count how many I should buy: two daughters, three sisters, one mother, one secretary, how many friends? I cannot think. I buy only six crosses, knowing it won't be enough. I cannot bring myself to buy more. I hate to feel like a tourist stocking up on postcards when these are crosses bought on the day I touched the rock of Golgotha and wept at the Stone of Anointing.

On impulse, I buy figs from a street-seller. I've never had fresh figs before. They're plump and as purple as eggplant, streaked with green. They feel alive, and are delicious.

By the time we get back to Saint George's, it's past five o'clock. We're supposed to attend a vespers service immediately. But my pilgrim feet hurt. I'm thirsty and hot: I feel like I've been thirsty and hot for days. At vespers we will not be allowed even a water bottle. So Kyle and I detour to the cathedral courtyard for a different sort of vespers. Taybeh beer is made in a Christian village near Ramallah. Drinking it will be an act of solidarity — like intercessory prayer. We raise our bottles to the Christians of Palestine.

I say to Kyle, "I suppose, if it's possible to get drunk on God, Jerusalem is the place to do it."

"Amen," he agrees.

"Honestly, I feel a bit punch-drunk," I say.

"Would that be the Spirit doing the punching?"

We laugh at the image. But the truth is that all of us gorged

ourselves on spiritual experiences today. We were spiritual glut-
tons. Does that make us pilgrims or tourists? I want to slow this
pilgrimage down and allow room for the Spirit. But I want to
drink it all in because I may never be able to come back. I don't
want to miss a thing.

🐚   🐚   🐚

Dinner is chicken and saffron rice. Then there's a meeting of the
whole group in the lecture room to share the day's experience.

"Where did you experience a communion of the saints?" is
the question.

People describe moments of connection with pilgrims past
and present. I think about my connections. My experience at the
Western Wall would seem an unlikely sort of communion. But
weren't the Jewish mother, the baby, and I all connected by our
hope in God? And the Crusader crosses, those strange acts of
devotion. I didn't want to claim my connection to their bloody
history, their savagery. But aren't we connected by folly? Perhaps
future generations will see our folly more clearly than we do.

Michael describes an experience of the Spirit while in the
marble tomb, a sense of the Spirit right there beside him, which
made him appreciate the enormity of Jesus' crucifixion. I had
been kneeling beside Michael and hadn't known he was moved.
How intimate, how personal these holy experiences are! It's hard
to give voice to them even to the person beside you.

After the meeting, the smaller documentary group has a brief
worship service on the rooftop. Jessica leads us, using some David
Crowder music and the text about the healing of Blind Bartimaeus,
which forms the basis of the Jesus Prayer. My very long day has
come full circle. To close, we stand and take turns praying. It is
sweet, even as our language betrays our doctrinal differences.

After the Amen, Brian produces a bottle of wine and small glass
cups like jelly jars. We pour the wine and drink, still standing in
our prayer circle. The lights of Jerusalem are spread at our feet. The
moment feels sacramental, and no one moves to break the circle.

CHAPTER 10

Birth and Death

I am the gate for the sheep.

JOHN 10:7

T ODAY IS TUESDAY. Bethlehem.
When I go down to breakfast, the documentary group
is sitting at a table, looking dispirited.

"What's wrong?"

Jessica sighs. "Tomatoes and cucumbers are all right, I guess.
But for every meal? For breakfast?"

"Let's just hope they have something different for lunch,"
Ashley says with a forced smile. "Not chicken."

"Why bother hoping?" Charlie says, emphatically. "Lunch
and supper will be the same as always: chicken and yellow rice.
And yellow — *why?*" Charlie's drawl gives the word "why" two
syllables.

"That's from saffron — " JoAnne begins to explain.

"Believe me, you don't want to know why it's yellow," Michael
says, and everybody laughs.

🐛 🐛 🐛

After breakfast, Stephen begins his lecture with a simple question:
"Was Jesus born in Bethlehem?" Warm, dry air wafts through an

open window, and I want to get up and look out at Jerusalem. "There are some good reasons to answer, 'Probably not.'" Some of my fellow pilgrims shift audibly in their seats, telegraphing discomfort. I squiggle deeper into my molded plastic chair and open my notebook.

The earliest writings in the New Testament are the Epistles of Paul, and the apostle never mentions Bethlehem. In fact, Paul mentions Jesus' birth only in two passing references to the fact that Jesus was born of flesh. Usually, when Paul talks about Jesus, it is "him crucified." Perhaps Paul preached about the birth elsewhere and that record has been lost to us. Or perhaps Paul didn't know the tradition that Jesus was born in Bethlehem.

The earliest Gospel is Mark's, and he is silent on Jesus' birth. Luke's famous account of the census — Mary and Joseph's journey from Nazareth to Bethlehem, which we read and hear every Christmas — is problematic because there is no historical record of the census that Luke mentions. Did this census, in fact, ever happen? Stephen's voice underscores the improbability. Another wrinkle: No one disputes that Nazareth was Jesus' hometown. Was Nazareth, then, where he was actually born? Still another wrinkle: There is a second Bethlehem in Galilee. Which one is the correct location?

"Was Jesus born in Bethlehem?" Stephen asks again. "The question is more difficult to answer than might appear. Yet there are some good reasons for us to answer, 'Probably yes.'" Again, there is shifting in the seats.

For openers, not just one but two Gospels, Matthew and Luke, record the Nativity as taking place in Bethlehem. So the Bethlehem tradition is very old, dating back to the first century, perhaps even before the written record, and is well-developed in the earliest literature. As for Bethlehem versus Nazareth, that conundrum isn't really so difficult. We all understand that a birthplace and a hometown can be different places.

Stephen presents scholar Raymond Brown's suggestion that Christology developed retrospectively, beginning with the cross, and moving back toward the birth. "The idea of objective history is a Western Enlightenment idea that we often mistakenly apply to Scripture." I glance at Shane and notice that he's scowling. My heart softens. Stephen's lecture is not new material to me, but I remember when I learned all this and found it threatening. Biblical criticism is a lot to absorb, especially if you're already overloaded by the sights and smells and people of the Holy Land.

"The upshot?" Stephen says. "After you balance faith and history — the Gospels, the Epistles, and the tradition — Bethlehem is a reasonable answer to the question of where was Jesus born."

Then come some easy facts. *Beth-lehem* means "house of bread" in Hebrew. The fourteen-point star is a symbol of Bethlehem because Jesus' genealogy is recounted in three groups of fourteen generations in Matthew 1:17. It is a pleasure to write down these undisputed facts.

We board the bus for the five-mile trip to Bethlehem. As usual, we documentary folk sit in the back of the bus. "So, what did you think of the lecture?" JoAnne asks Shane.

"Why do you ask?" he responds.

"Because it reminded me of seminary, I guess. It's not every day you hear a lecture like that. So I wondered what that was like for you."

"Why? Because I haven't been to seminary?" Shane says. "I'll tell you what. I don't think any of this is as hard as people make it out to be."

"The Bible is compli — " JoAnne begins, but Shane cuts her off.

"Maybe I'll never go to seminary. I don't have to. I'm already doing ministry." Shane's voice has an edge.

"Good for you," says JoAnne. "You're doing what you want to do."

There's a little lull as people let go of the conversation and turn back to their seatmates. "When you went to seminary," I ask Michael, "did they dismantle everything you thought you believed?"

He grins. "They sure did."

"It's good to know the Lutherans do that, too," I say.

Stephen gets on the bus's loudspeaker to alert us to the fact that we're passing through Gehenna Valley, which was the city's original garbage dump. In the Bible it's referred to as a place that's constantly burning, a place where the outcasts scavenged a living. It's significant because it gave birth to Scripture's Gehenna/hell imagery. The bus windows are open, but I don't notice any overpowering odors, which is disappointing. I have a good nose and had hoped to catch the stench of hell itself. But I've smelled much worse in New York City during garbage workers' strikes.

The bus winds through city streets and then suburbs, never leaving greater Jerusalem before we arrive at the Wall of Separation between Israel and the West Bank. We are armed with our passports. A teenager in a dark green uniform and black beret boards the bus carrying a rifle in both hands. He strides down the aisle, swinging his head from side to side for a cursory glance at our papers. He doesn't stop to examine anything. When he passes me, I notice that his cheeks are peach-fuzzed.

The bus gets the go-ahead and begins to move. Camera Michael scrambles in front of me to film out my window. We both strain and crane as we roll past the barrier. The Wall stretches twice as high as our bus and casts a long shadow, both literally and figuratively. It is an obstruction that demarcates inside from outside, Israeli from Palestinian, citizen from noncitizen. My heart beats faster when I see a large group of soldiers and a tank at the ready. I wonder if the young men in uniform like being on the side they're on, or if they feel locked into this conflict in complicated ways.

In Bethlehem we stop to pick up our guide for the day: Sam, a Palestinian Christian. The staff at Saint George's always hires a Palestinian guide when the pilgrim tours cross into the Occupied Territories. They do this partly as a courtesy, because this is Palestinian land; but they also do it as an act of justice: the people here are desperate for employment. The Second Intifada in 2000 decimated the tourist business — it declined by some 90 percent.

The bus heads to the Shepherds' Field on the eastern side of Bethlehem, grinding gears as the driver downshifts on a long,

steep hill. On either side of the street are boarded-up businesses
and barred windows. There are very few people out and about.
Sam tells us that the population of Bethlehem is currently 28,000, *in Palestine*
and nearly everyone is unemployed. He gives us the religious
breakdown: 70 percent are Muslim and 30 percent are Christian,
although both groups may include large numbers of atheists.

I remember Tercier, the atheist we encountered at the Monastery of the Flagellation. He was from Bethlehem, and told
us the joke about Jesus being trapped on the wrong side of the
Wall. I recorded that joke just as I now record Sam's statistics. I
tell myself that I'm writing down facts to use in sermons later;
but in truth I'm trying to capture this experience so that I can
process it later. I want to appreciate each point of view. There
is so much I don't know, and the statistics are the least of it. To
me the real growth comes from meeting Tercier, and Sam, from
passing through the shadow of the Wall, from seeing everything
here firsthand.

Sam explains that the Shepherds' Field is the setting for two
well-known Bible stories. As I hoped, he mentions Ruth and
Boaz. I love that story, and I delight in being Ruth's namesake.
She was so brave! I want to have access to her courage and resolve. She was powerless because she was a woman, as well as
an outsider, a Moabitess. Yet she ended up in the covenant line
because she gave birth to a child who was one of Jesus' forebears.
She is named in Matthew's genealogy, the passage immortalized
in that fourteen-point star we'll be seeing in the Church of the
Nativity. Certainly that makes her a chosen one.

Ruth's combination of outside-ness and chosen-ness has always
struck a deep chord in me. These two poles are also important to
my life story. Because I was born into an ethnically tight faith
community with a strong theology of the covenant, I always felt
chosen. We were all chosen, my whole Dutch Reformed community — born into that covenant and chosen by God. How I
would like to talk to a Jewish person about this sense of chosen-
ness, which seems to be a double-edged sword! But I have no
idea how to begin that conversation. Besides, I was chosen, but I

was also a woman, and because of that I had a certain role to play. When I felt called into ministry, I moved outside the acceptable boundaries of the community. I had no choice but to leave the womb of my early world and become an outsider.

Palestinian Sam is quoting a familiar Scripture passage: "In that region there were shepherds abiding in the field. . . ." And the whole busload of us shouts in unison, "Keeping watch over their flocks by night." We grin at each other as the bus lurches down the hill.

Finally we arrive. The Shepherds' Field is rocky and steeply sloped. We go single file, making a hairpin turn around a precipitous drop, which exposes the entrance to a cave. Single file down eight or so stone steps between rough rock walls. The steps are spaced evenly enough to have been hewn.

By the dim light I can see that the cave is made entirely of stone. There are niches chiseled into the wall here and there. In certain spots the walls and ceiling are black with soot. I imagine the fires that people burned in those places to chase the chill away. One "room" has enough space for us to gather. Sam explains that this empty pocket occurred naturally in the hillside, and over the centuries has been enlarged.

This is a sheep fold, used to shelter flocks at night. The cave protects sheep from wild animals and also from cold. Since a couple hundred sheep can fit into the cave, four or five shepherds and their flocks share the space. The shepherds rotate keeping watch at the single entrance. The shepherd on duty is called "the Door" or "the Gate." This familiar Scripture reference, heard in this unfamiliar place, slices into me with new power. This underground cave is far removed from a Sunday school picture of a white-robed shepherd sitting on a well-placed rock contemplating the landscape while holding a picturesque staff.

"Jesus said, 'I am the gate for the sheep.'" In the shadowy cave, Sam is standing in a shaft of light, and I want to go throw my arms around him and kiss his cheek. Maybe his white hair reminds me of my father, or maybe he has become my father by leading me to something precious about my faith, a faith that I've certainly inhabited my whole life but am embracing anew.

We wander around, and Sam tells us that we are like the sheep, referring to the way we're mixing freely inside the cave. That's what sheep would do. Each shepherd has his own call, and the sheep respond to it. Sheep are herd animals. They like to be together, and that makes them much easier to herd than goats. Goats don't bunch together, and they don't listen. "Goats like to wander and plunder," Sam says.

Maybe I'm more goat than sheep. I'm definitely some sort of wayward animal. Even here in the Holy Land I've felt the pull to do things I shouldn't do. The tradition in which I grew up would simply say this was my unworthiness. But I'm starting to think it's something different. I am no more or less unworthy than anybody else. Still, I'm a human being and have choices to make — all the time. Something seems to be shifting in my theology on a visceral level.

Sam is pointing out a stone trough like the one Mary used as a manger. I picture Mary placing Jesus in that furrow of rock. Wouldn't a stone manger be cold? I remember the tombs from yesterday, deep inside the Church of the Holy Sepulchre: the dirty oven tomb and the clean marble tomb. Both were cold. Whether natural rock or worked marble, stone is cold. For the first time it really hits me that Jesus not only ended his life lying on stone, but began his life that way. Our Christmas card pictures are downright cozy in their contrast to reality. What a chilly reception for a divine being who voluntarily entered our flesh. Flesh is warm, yet only for a brief span. And to think within that span, such coldness! I think of how often I've preached on Jesus' incarnation, and how little I understand it.

Sam talks more about shepherds. He explains that the business of the town of Bethlehem was to provide sheep for the Temple at Jerusalem, only five miles distant. Masses of sheep were born and raised here in Bethlehem, only to be slaughtered on the altar in Jerusalem. It's not hard to find the metaphor there: Jesus is not only the Good Shepherd, but also the Lamb of God.

Sam explains that shepherds played a unique role in Temple culture. They were crucial to Temple life because they provided an essential commodity; yet, at the same time, they were outcasts, excluded from Temple functions. They were sinners, ritually unclean. These were, of course, the holiness laws coming into effect; these laws also excluded Gentiles and women. Shepherds were unclean because they touched sick animals, excrement, and blood. They were stained. The irony is clear: the shepherds provided the means for other people's sins to be forgiven via blood sacrifice, but they themselves had no access to forgiveness. Jesus is the Good Shepherd. Perhaps the metaphor works because he didn't need forgiveness like an ordinary shepherd.

Someone in the group asks whether the shepherds owned their sheep. "No," Sam says. "Most of the shepherds were hired hands." He goes on to explain that it was often the Sadducees who owned the sheep, as part of their role in maintaining Temple operations. In fact, sheep were the greatest source of the Sadducees' wealth. Still, being a shepherd wasn't a bad job. Shepherds were paid relatively well, and often owners and shepherds worked together for a lifetime and passed their positions to the next generation. "The shepherd's well-being," says Sam, "was tied to the well-being of the sheep."

Now someone asks about stone itself, and Sam talks about "generativity." That's another word we don't use much. Sam says that a cave is a symbol for the womb, embodying safety and nurturing. He elaborates on what we heard yesterday: cave theology. This was first proposed by Eusebius in the fourth century. Not only did Jesus' body spend its first and last moments on a rock, but all the pivotal biblical stories about him — birth/death/resurrection/ascension — happened on a rock or in a rock cave.

Sam talks about swaddling cloths, how they were used for both newborns and corpses, and thus encapsulate birth and death in one image. This is not a new tidbit for me; in fact, I've used it in sermons. But when I hear this while standing in a rock cave — both birthplace and tomb — the poignancy of the image hits me almost physically. I suck in my breath. Jesus was wrapped in death rags from the moment he drew breath. You have to wonder why he did it! Why would a deity bother with the mess and inconvenience of flesh?

Sam segues into leadership: "God often used shepherding as a way to train leaders. A good shepherd is a good leader because he has to search out the good lands, has to negotiate with other shepherds, has to be attentive to his flock." That concise description brings me up short. For years I've rebelled internally against the image of pastor as shepherd — even though the two words are related — because the image seems clichéd, both sanitized and overused. Perhaps I've been influenced by the sentimental hymn arrangements of Psalm 23, or the Sunday school pictures that show a clean white lamb slung around the shepherd's neck, but the pastor as shepherd seems to suggest that the job of a pastor is primarily reactive, to scoop people up when they fall. Standing in the shepherd's cave in Bethlehem, I suddenly realize that this notion severely shortchanges the biblical image.

"Can you name some leaders who were shepherds?" Sam asks.

We call them out: Abraham, Isaac, Jacob, Moses, David.

"Shepherding is good training, like fishing," Sam says. "Shall I tell you about that?"

Ashley shouts, "Preach it, Sam!" and our group applauds.

So he does. In a few sentences Sam talks about fishermen, how they learn to be quiet and stay out of sight. How they must know their fish well to know what kind of bait to use.

JoAnne whispers to me, "We'll be in Galilee in two days, you know."

My heart fills with anticipation. Already I'm approaching that place, which I've never seen, with new eyes.

Then it's time to leave the embrace of the cave and board the bus. We are going up the long hill to see "the actual place where Jesus was born."

....

CHAPTER II

Love Is Difficult

For now we see in a mirror, dimly, but then we will see face to face.
Now I know only in part; then I will know fully, even as I have
been fully known. And now faith, hope, and love abide, these three;
and the greatest of these is love.

1 CORINTHIANS 13:12-13

THE CHURCH OF the Nativity is one of the sites established
by Constantine in the fourth century. His mother, Helena,
was pretty sure it was the authentic place of Jesus' birth, since
people had been worshiping there for centuries. Helena had a
church built at the exact location where the actual manger stood.
That structure was destroyed in the sixth century and rebuilt.
Along the way, the Orthodox argued with the Catholics, who
argued with the Armenians. The result was that two sanctuaries were built over one holy site. Dual sanctuaries. Dueling
sanctuaries.

Stephen explains that the building's disagreeable history
doesn't end there. In the eleventh century, the Crusaders rode
into Bethlehem to bring Christ to the masses through brute force.
They did some good things for the church building — such as
enlarging it. But their presence also created some unusual problems. People would sometimes ride into the church on a beast
— horse, donkey, camel — charge right up to the altar, and grab
some holy object, then gallop off. It is unclear to me who did
this, or why, or exactly what they would grab. Was it common
theft or something more? The Crusaders solved the problem by

adding a new entrance with a doorway low enough to keep out mounted marauders. They called it the Door of Humility.

This story is told to explain why we must bend low as we pass through this door. In fact, we must bend from the waist, as if we are entering a cave. It's a pleasing metaphor, but I doubt whether it was, or is, effective pedagogically. The spiritual lesson of humility cannot be taught through architecture.

There's a more recent chapter of this building's history, also violent, that needs to be told. In April 2002, armed Palestinians forced their way into this church. Using two hundred nuns and priests as shields, they refused to surrender their position for thirty-nine days. The world paid attention, and there was great pressure on the Israelis not to destroy this holy site. Ultimately, the Palestinians surrendered.

Surely, if there is any place in the world that should be bathed in blissful love, it should be the place where Jesus was born. But Bethlehem is not a sweet place. Perhaps that's fitting: Jesus wasn't born to bring "niceness." Jesus was born to inaugurate the kingdom of God. The world was so allergic to that kingdom that they tried to stamp him out. It isn't surprising that the raw ingredients of sacred presence are too powerful and intoxicating to be sweet.

Faith is full of such paradoxes. I think how, for years, my family ended our mealtime prayers with a simple chant: "God is great, God is good, let us thank him for our food." Saying God is great means that God is all-powerful. Saying God is good means that God is all-loving. We experience God's power and love through the simple gifts we receive, like food on the table. But sometimes there isn't food on the table, so to speak. Why is that so? As some theologians have put it: If God is so great, why is everything not so good?

If maturity is the ability to hold two conflicting ideas in your head without your brain exploding, spiritual maturity is the ability to wrap your head around God's being both good and great without your faith exploding. The truth is that God's goodness and greatness present a paradox, and rather than try to understand that paradox, we must simply stand under it. Within that paradox is the space where we humans live our lives: exercising our free will, making choices, and experiencing the results of our choices, and the choices of others.

Seminary taught me to resolve this paradox with a doctrine that we Presbyterians are particularly fond of: the sovereignty of God. That's what theology does: it gives us labels to contain things we can't explain. I've drawn on these labels as I've written sermons, to help name the unnameable. Yet, standing in this open plaza in Bethlehem, in front of a church that marks both God's incarnation and human mayhem, the poignancy of these paradoxes deepens.

The sun shines brightly on the Church of the Nativity. Our group is clustered around Stephen in a section of the paved courtyard; similar groups dot the plaza. At the edges of each group, street-sellers ply their wares. Out of the corner of my eye I notice some sellers waiting near our group. Sam is explaining that in some places we will be able to see the original mosaic floor. Underneath this church is the original cave where Jesus was born, and the exact spot where his manger stood. Each time Sam says "original," his voice underscores the word.

As the group breaks up to move into the church, street-sellers swarm us, pushing postcards into our hands and pleading. "Please, I have five children at home, please to buy." Many of them have arms draped in stone necklaces, which they swing before us. One man has Palestinian scarves that catch my eye. "My name is Hakim," he says.

We enter the church and peer at a roped-off piece of mosaic floor. It seems very dark and dirty, and I want to call for a scrub bucket.

There is a funeral going on in the Orthodox sanctuary. The top of the coffin is propped in the corner. It bears a large, Crusader-style cross and seems like a stage prop. But it isn't. I'm used to caskets with closed lids, death one step more remote than this. I want to glimpse the coffin but can't because the sanctuary is full of people standing.

We pilgrims must walk alongside a railing that separates us

from the mourners, which we do respectfully. There's a silent traffic jam as we stoop through a narrow doorway one at a time. We continue single file down a long grade to the cave where Helena built her shrine so many centuries ago. It feels like we are deep underground when we come at last to the shrine at the manger. Set in a slab of marble is the fourteen-point star. Hanging over this star is a row of lamps. I drop a shekel in a box and light a long taper, which I anchor in a bed of sand. Then I kneel and pray for the peace of Bethlehem.

We head out of the cave through a passageway in the opposite direction. Along the way — as if we might need another reminder that joy is never unmixed with sorrow — we pass the Chapel of the Innocents, which commemorates Herod's order to kill all Jewish boys under the age of two in his attempt to kill the baby Jesus. This is the morning-after-Christmas story that doesn't get as much press.

We crowd into another chapel that once housed the bones of the church father Jerome. Sam tells us about Jerome, who lived in Bethlehem from 386 to 420 CE, and translated Scripture into Latin, possibly in this very room. The rock walls are beautiful in their irregularity, hewn by hand. Jessica whispers to me, "Now this is some kind of study." I nod my agreement. We writers understand the pull of contemplative space.

The passageway continues up into the other sanctuary, Saint Catherine's, which is Catholic, a mere 120 years old. We are given a few minutes alone. I go forward to kneel and listen to the words of the red-robed priest who is celebrating the Eucharist: "We proclaim your death, O Lord, and profess your resurrection, until you come again. When we eat this bread and drink this cup, we proclaim your death, O Lord, until you come again."

As I listen to these ancient words, it occurs to me that this sacrament — like everything about this Church of the Nativity — points to the glimmering threshold between life and death. In this sanctuary, worshipers celebrate Jesus' death and resurrection; in the other sanctuary, worshipers witness a funeral; both sanctuaries like legs straddle the place where Jesus was born.

Birth and death. On the one hand, birthing and burying are common human experiences, going on all the time. Yet for the main actors — and the persons watching and waiting — they are pivotal and life-altering. A birthing bed or a deathbed are each a holy place where we wait with bated breath for the threshold to be crossed. This sanctuary is the same. We see that God is on both sides of the threshold and that indeed the doorway between these realities is more translucent and temporary than we know. For a brief, holy moment, I can glimpse both directions at once — toward life and toward death — and feel God's presence. My fingers grasp the wooden pew, my feet are anchored on the stone floor, my eyes rest on the lifted communion chalice, and time ceases. Eternity surrounds me.

Someone taps me on the shoulder. My sense of time isn't good in the best of circumstances. As a pilgrim, I'm a complete time failure. Why do I even wear a watch?

We begin to walk down a long hill to the bus. Along the way, I decide to buy one of the headscarves, wanting to express solidarity with the Palestinians. I see the street-seller named Hakim and call his name. He responds with delight and comes running. He knows he has me.

Now I must decide between red and black. Red is Bedouin; black is Palestinian. I try to picture one of them draped across the communion table in my church. I dither — rubbing the fabric between my fingers — until I decide I want to buy both. I will try to haggle as I should, but it won't be easy. I offer to buy two for the price of one as Kyle and I start walking toward the bus. Hakim trails beside me, and Camera Michael shows up, camera rolling. Hakim protests that he has no profit margin at all; I must pay a little more. I am no good at this. I don't know if what he says about profit margins is true, but I do know that I am rich to him. I flew here in a plane, didn't I? I finger the scarves again.

"Excellent quality," he promises.

We negotiate the price from 80 shekels ($20) each to two for 120 shekels ($30). I have left my money on the bus, so Kyle loans me some. When the transaction is finished, Hakim continues walking beside me, companionably. I'm surprised. All around are other tourists, potential targets.

"What state are you from?" he asks.

"Virginia," I say. "Do you know it?"

"Is it near New Jersey?"

I nod, and he shakes his head sorrowfully. "I will never go there. Never! A girl from New Jersey broke my heart." He beats a closed fist against his chest.

I'm glad Camera Michael is filming. I love Hakim's theatrics. I play along. "I'm especially sorry," I tell him, "since I am also a girl from New Jersey."

Now his shock is unfeigned. "Really?"

"Really," I say. "I lived there for ten years. I went to high school there."

"Have you broken a heart there?" he asks dejectedly.

"Not in New Jersey. Not that I know of."

He shakes his head again, as if he is an old man and all of his grandchildren have disappointed him. "If someone breaks your heart, it is broken forever. Love is forever. You cannot help it."

I commiserate: "Yes, love is difficult." We walk down the hill toward the bus — with me clutching my two scarves and him trailing an armload. We both wag our heads over love, then part with a firm handshake beside the noisy bus.

CHAPTER 12

The Hope

How very good and pleasant it is when kindred live together in unity!

PSALM 133:1

T HE BUS TAKES us to a Palestinian refugee camp called Deheshieh (duh-HAY-shuh). We are served lunch in a community building that is owned by the United Nations. The food is typical of what we've been served before: hummus, cucumbers, tomatoes, pita bread. The main dish is served by the plate: a large mound of white rice topped with a bone. The bone has a knob of dark meat, probably lamb. My body seems to be toying with a case of what Stephen politely calls "Herod's Revenge," so I offer my meat to Brian and eat enough of the rice to get by.

After lunch we're given a tour of the camp. Our guide's name is Jihad Ramadan. Now there's a name that communicates! He looks to be in his early twenties, a compactly built man with pronounced muscles, shiny black hair, and olive skin. His face is beautiful, lit with fervor. A pack of cigarettes bulges in the pocket of his tight-fitting T-shirt, which is red, white, and blue. I suspect that he isn't wearing those colors to honor the U.S. flag.

He speaks with impassioned eloquence. Deheshieh is one of fifty-eight refugee camps. In fact, it was the first camp, established in 1948. From 1948 to 1967, the West Bank was owned by Jordan; but in 1967 the United Nations began to rent this land from Jordan for a term of ninety-nine years. All housing and services are managed by the U.N. This camp covers one square kilometer and houses 11,000 people. That density is shocking, even to me, living in densely populated northern Virginia. But I am stuck on another fact. This has been a refugee camp from 1948 until now? Doesn't "camp" imply that it's temporary? How many generations have already been raised here? Being a refugee isn't the temporary condition I naïvely imagine it to be.

There is one clinic with one doctor for the entire camp. One doctor sees 280 patients per week. Again, I attempt calculations in my head: Is that fifty-five patients per day, some five minutes per patient?

Jihad has no trouble projecting his voice over the group. It's obvious that he has given this tour many times. The statistics flow, well-rehearsed, but emotion makes his voice raw. He's talking about medication. Basically, it isn't available. Sixty percent of the people living in this camp are children — 6,000 of them. There are fifty students per classroom. In spite of that dismal statistic, Deheshieh is the most educated of the camps. I notice that many people have their faces scrunched up. I realize that mine is scrunched up too, from the sun, from concentrating on such crude facts.

"Do people here work?" someone asks.

"Basically, no," Jihad answers. "There are no jobs, and you can't get to Jerusalem."

"But isn't it only a few miles away?"

"Isolationism by the Israelis!" Jihad shouts, then walks on.

We pass walls covered with posters picturing young men, like mug shots only more flattering. "Martyrs," Jihad calls out, gesturing to them. He stops and assembles the group to announce, "During the First Intifada, there were thirteen martyrs from this camp. During the Second Intifada, thirty-five martyrs."

He recites these statistics in the automatic way that I recite my daughters' birthdates when necessary — facts so much a part of me that I don't need to think about them.

"What, exactly, is a martyr?" Ashley asks me. It sounds like an elementary question, but I don't know how Jihad would answer. Another pilgrim repeats Ashley's question in a loud voice.

Jihad answers, "A martyr is any person killed by an Israeli soldier."

I wonder whether this definition includes suicide bombers. I'm sympathetic toward the Palestinians, yet it seems obvious that for the Israelis this definition could be reversed.

"Martyrs are killed in cold blood, including children. They lose everything, even the hope."

Jihad's use of the article "the" in front of "hope" feels profound. It underscores that hope is a commodity: it can be given and taken away. It is a necessity, like water and food and medical care. It is precious. It is the one commodity that the church has a unique mandate to dispense.

Jihad talks about curfews. During curfew no one can leave home. Soldiers come and impose the curfew with loudspeakers. Curfew can last for twenty-four hours, or a week, or a month — they never say. It is imposed until it is lifted. The longest curfew was imposed in 1991, during the First Gulf War, when there were forty-eight consecutive days of curfew.

"During the Church of the Nativity invasion," Jihad continues, "there was a forty-day curfew. All of that time, people could not get food. An old man getting a basket of bread was killed by thirty-six bullets from a tank."

I can see the old man in my mind, clutching his loaf of bread, gunned down by Israeli soldiers. I can taste the hatred that pours from Jihad.

Children are following us, curious, and we pilgrims take pictures. They mug for the cameras. Two boys stick particularly close. One boy is skinny, the other round, like any American twosome. Jihad describes the ball games that children play in the streets, and how they adapt because the streets are narrow, the buildings close.

"There are no playgrounds," he tells us. "There are soldiers and checkpoints. There is no childhood."

An old woman stands and watches us. She wears a scarf on her head like a babushka and carries an empty tin basin. She catches my eye and waves. I wave back, snap her picture. The pastor in me wants to sit down for a home visit. A cup of tea would be lovely. I'd ask about her kids and grandkids, read a Psalm, pray with her. I can imagine her soft, worn hands in mine.

"We didn't choose to be political people. Politics chose us," Jihad says.

Now he talks about water. There is no water in the summer, and no electricity in the winter. There are five wells in Bethlehem, yet all water is controlled by the Israelis, and most goes to the Israeli settlers, even though they are building on Palestinian land. The allotments are grossly inequitable: a five-liter allotment per Palestinian, a five-cubic-meter allotment per Israeli. What does that look like? Five liters meets basic needs. Five cubic meters means swimming pools and gardens.

"What about electricity?" someone asks.

"It is available," Jihad answers. "The problem is where to get the money to pay for it."

Someone asks about the relationships with the Israelis, especially the Orthodox Jews.

Jihad spits. "Hasidim treat Palestinians lower than dogs."

Perhaps that's why he begins talking about toilets. There are no toilets in the housing. Instead, there is one public toilet for every twenty-five rooms. There is one family in each room, no matter the size of the family. So there are at least a hundred people using each toilet. Virtually everyone in this camp is Muslim, and the women are conservative. They do not want to be seen walking to the public toilet. I don't understand all the nuances, but comprehend the result: Women do not use the toilets in the afternoon. This causes more health problems.

"Everything about the housing is a problem — especially that the Israelis like to destroy it!"

The Israelis believe in collective punishment, an atrocity they learned from the British, who imposed it during the years of the British Mandate. For each Palestinian who acts in defiance, the punishments ripple out against dozens and even hundreds of people. When a home is destroyed by soldiers, it doesn't affect just one family — it affects a whole neighborhood.

"Do they use bulldozers?" someone asks.

I appreciate her question. The Episcopalians, like the Presbyterians, are debating whether to divest in certain companies that sell to Israel. One company is Caterpillar, which makes heavy equipment. It feels good to be part of a progressive denomination that seeks justice.

"No," Jihad replies. "Explosives."

So it doesn't even matter. My denomination tries to do one thing for justice for the Palestinians, and that one thing is beside the point.

"The soldiers come with loudspeakers. 'You have thirty minutes to get out!' Then they blow the house up. They do this to anyone they don't like. They punish many people instead of one."

"What do you think of the United States?" someone asks.

"In general, government is bullshit," Jihad answers.

"What about Europe?"

"The U.S. shows solidarity with Europe, and they are all controlled by the media," he replies. "The media hate us."

"What about the churches?"

"We are not looking for charity. We are looking for solidarity." Jihad stops, seeming to notice that Ashley is crying. He looks right at her, contemptuously, and says, "Crying is not enough. If you want to help, challenge the policy of your government, and we will achieve our rights."

Ashley wipes her tears, hardens her face.

I wish Jihad hadn't said that. I wish he would realize that he's telling us things we'd rather not know, would understand that tears are part of the process of building solidarity. Before people take on a cause, they must be convicted of its importance, and the gateway to that conviction is emotion. Each of us pilgrims must decide if we will carry a burden for Jihad and his people. I roll his name over in my mouth again so I can make peace with it. Jihad. I look around this un-temporary camp of concrete-block buildings, tiny alleyways, and graffiti proclaiming "Stop the Wall!" Who knows who I would be if I had grown up here.

We return to the same building where we began — it is the only public building — and enter the first floor. We file into a single room that's smaller than most of the classrooms I know. It cannot handle our group. There is already a small group of medical students present, who are introduced to us. They're part of an international team here to work with the children. They look haggard and dusty.

We're here to see an exhibit about what Palestine used to look like. "This was created to educate the children," Jihad explains. The entire exhibit is maybe one-fifth the size of my daughter's eighth-grade science fair. A few posters describe land formations and native species of birds, animals, and plants. My eye catches on a map of "depopulated villages" that poses the question: "Is there room now for the Palestinians to return home?"

The answer is in bold type: "Yes."

All of a sudden it strikes me: This conflict is about land. Holy land. How have I not fully comprehended this before? This is the on-the-ground problem that I only thought about theoretically before I made this pilgrimage. That I barely dared to think about theoretically! But it is an unavoidable problem.

The pilgrims are looking at the exhibits and some embroidered items that are for sale, which the women and girls of the camp make. The prices seem very low, so I select two embroidered shoulder bags for 60 shekels ($15) each. They will make nice gifts, and I want to support the camp. I don't know how else to respond to this entrenched suffering. Some women in our group dicker with Jihad, who has pulled a pad with carbon copies from his back pocket, and is writing up receipts. One woman raises her voice, trying to get him to lower a price. Eventually she shakes her head and stalks away angry.

Ashley whispers to me, "Do you think she mixed up shekels and dollars?"

"I wonder," I say. "Why else?"

After a day full of heat and heated words, I'm eager for a few minutes alone in the air-conditioned bus. As I exit the building, a Palestinian man lays his hand on my forearm. I pause, and he plunks a hat on my head, then gestures for payment. I shake my head No and move away. He stops me again, touching my arm. As I take the hat off, he plunks another on my head. Now I have one hat on my head and another in my hand. The man talks and gestures loudly, as if I have wronged him. I am immobilized.

From the bus, Camera Michael notices my dilemma. He approaches the man and speaks roughly. The man ignores him, and Michael repeats himself, his voice escalating. The man won't take the hats back, so I throw them in the dust, even though I'd rather not. But I must play my part in this game. Michael takes my arm and escorts me to the bus. I'm flooded with relief. It's been years since I felt so vulnerable.

People are straggling back onto the bus. Someone wonders aloud whether we'll have the opportunity to buy ice cream. The conversation veers to ice cream's companion food: pizza.

I don't volunteer anything. My mind stays fixed on the encounter in the dust.

The bus finally begins to move. As we head to the checkpoint in the Wall, Stephen points out a brand-new Israeli settlement taking up a whole hilltop in the distance, white and clean in the sun. There's a historical site he would like to show us: the tomb of Rachel, who is buried here because she died giving birth to Benjamin on the road to Bethlehem. Unfortunately, the tomb is between two sections of the wall, and is politically difficult — so we cannot stop.

Instead, Stephen reads a poem aloud: "Journey of the Magi" by T. S. Eliot. One line becomes imprinted on my memory: "I had seen birth and death. But had thought they were different." Stephen clicks the microphone off, and I'm glad for a time to be silent and consider birth and death. Swaddling cloths, wrapping both a newborn and a corpse. Rock — cold, yet generative. Palestinian families multiplying in the confines of tiny housing units. Rachel, giving birth to Benjamin before she died.

Sometimes I wish the kingdom of God would just come

already. Maybe then we'd be done with all this mess of incarnation! Unless incarnation itself will be made perfect. That's a
lovely possibility, a world where birth and death will roll along in
perfect rhythm, as they do in the plant world. Today we paused
on the threshold between this life and the life that is to come.
I'm still heady with that brief glimpse of liminal space. Maybe
the kingdom of God is pure liminality, straddling the past and
the future with such beauty and simplicity that our vision will
be unobstructed in both directions. Our joy will be without end.

Stephen picks up the microphone and begins to sing "Ten
Measures of Beauty" by Garth Hewitt. The words are simple
enough, and we all join him on the chorus:

> *Ten measures of beauty God gave to the world,*
> *nine to Jerusalem, one to the rest.*
> *Ten measures of sorrow God gave to the world,*
> *nine to Jerusalem, one to the rest.*
> *So, pray for the peace, pray for the peace,*
> *Pray for the peace of Jerusalem.*

This afternoon Brian wants to do a group interview, on-camera.
He wants us to discuss our reactions to Bethlehem, the refugee
camp, the political realities of the Israeli/Palestinian conflict,
and how all that affects our faith. The last time he tried to film a
group interview, it became a rather heated debate over how we
interpret Scripture, so I give him credit for being willing to try
again, especially with such a charged subject.

The cameramen set up under a couple of flowering trees on
Saint George's campus. Michael and Charlie show up late, in
a very silly mood. They crack jokes as the boom microphone is
adjusted over their heads. When everything is ready, Brian asks
if anyone has an opening comment.

JoAnne says, "My spiritual director gave me a piece of advice that was helpful today. I'd like to share it with you." She unrolls a well-worn scrap of paper and reads: "*Live in the middle of the conflict, knowing that you cannot fix a thing.* I thought about that today as we walked through that refugee camp. Because she's right — I can't fix this. But I can take it in. And maybe that's enough."

"Now we've seen it firsthand," Ashley agrees. "We haven't exactly lived it, but we've tasted it."

"It reminds me of the first day," Jessica says. "Stephen said that a tourist passes through the place, but the place passes through the pilgrim. Remember that?"

"How can I forget it?" Michael responds. "This place has been passing through me for days." As if on cue, both Michael and Charlie make farting noises. There's a moment of incredulity as the rest of us look at each other, wide-eyed. Then we burst into giggles.

"He's right," JoAnne says. "I haven't had a normal poop in days."

I nod in agreement.

"Don't worry," says Charlie. "Because tonight's menu is chicken and — "

"Yellow rice!" we all shout.

This strikes us as so hilarious that our giggling turns into laughter, which becomes so overpowering that we clutch our bellies. The day's emotions — sympathy and helplessness in the face of profound suffering — overflow in tears of laughter, which are simply another form of our earlier tears. It's a relief to feel the surfeit of emotions drain away.

Brian signals the cameramen to stop. "Let's not waste any more film," he says quietly. "This is part of pilgrimage too, but I think you'd have to be here to understand."

CHAPTER 13

Suspension

In my distress I cry to the LORD, that he may answer me.

PSALM 120:1

TODAY IS DESERT day. The bus departs before sunrise, so I don't bother to eat breakfast. I stare out the window as the sky lightens into pearl and wish I'd taken time for a cup of coffee, even that wretched Nescafé. It occurs to me that becoming a pilgrim has intensified my addiction to caffeine. That would have surprised me when I thought pilgrimage was like prayer, something that helped a person become less polluted. But now I know differently. Pilgrimage may be holy, but it's not particularly pure. For that matter, neither is prayer. Both are hard work — and messy. Both require sweat and tears. Coffee helps. Lubrication.

As the bus lumbers east, the desert's scraggly green growth peters out. All that's left is the beige of rock and sand. Even the sky becomes a blue so watery and washed out that it's almost beige. God must love beige. A land of milk and honey, yes, but to my eyes it's a land of beige and beige.

Why, out of all the possible palettes, would the Creator choose this one? I want to argue with God's color choice, but as a young child I was schooled not to question the divine, not even to quibble or joke. "Don't make light of holy things. Don't be presumptuous." So, when an unanswerable question arose, I

95

learned to prick and deflate it. I don't do that anymore, but it's
disconcerting that questions multiply. I'm still processing yesterday's trip to the refugee camp. Why did this Holy Land end up
in such a mess? Why do people treat other people inhumanely?
What's religion got to do with it? I want God to explain this to
me. Or better, I want God to fix it.

Maybe this urge to quarrel with God proves that I, too, am in
the grip of this Holy Land. The Hebrew patriarchs are famous
for taking God head-on. Perhaps the covenant gave them the
necessary status. Didn't Abraham argue with God over the fate
of Sodom? Didn't Jacob wrestle a blessing from an angel? Didn't
Moses negotiate the terms of his spokesperson deal with God?

The Jews have a tradition of arguing with God, and I feel
a bit envious. We Calvinists don't do that. We elevate God so
high that we dare not approach. Instead, we assert our adoptive
claim as God's elect, then scramble to prove ourselves worthy of
its benefits and blessings.

Will I still be a Calvinist when this pilgrimage is over? The
bus rolls along while my thoughts tumble. It's ironic that I want
to tussle with God over problems that started when people felt
they had some sort of special dispensation that allowed them to
tussle with God.

Most of the people in the bus are dozing or staring vaguely
out the windows at the few signs of life. Occasionally we pass a
primitive building, and I wonder if it shelters people or animals. I
look for evidence of vehicles, cook-fires, clotheslines. I see none.
The buildings seem too huddled to house people. Occasionally a
lone sheep or goat drifts across the sand, untended.

Someone shouts and points out the window. In the distance
an entire hillside is moving. As the bus gets closer, it seems that
the sand is flowing alongside us like a river. There's commotion
as people crowd to one side of the bus. The flowing hillside isn't
sand, but a herd of sheep, their rounded, wooly backs rippling
like water and parting around rocks like a current. Near the back
of the herd is a lone Bedouin, his red-and-white scarf a spot of
color. In a moment we've left the scene behind us. Just when we've

been lulled into thinking this is nothing but a boring desert, we are surprised and thrilled. This is what a pilgrimage is, this up-ending of what you think you know to be true.

The bus continues south. The land flattens, and I doze. As we approach the Dead Sea, I wake, just in time to see a grove of date palm trees, unexpected and flamboyant. These tall trees have orange nets strapped beneath their feathery umbrellas, like girdles, to protect heavy clusters of dates.

The enormous plateau of Masada is visible from a distance. It's a stunning formation, a geological oddity. Imagine you're an ant in a sandbox when a toddler, or some other God-like being, drops a gigantic, flat-topped rock next to you. What could you do with such an object?

Our guide for the day, Rula, is a Christian of Bedouin ancestry. Her long hair is light brown, settling on her shoulders with a curl. She is knowledgeable and well-spoken. Now she takes the microphone to give us some background before we arrive. She tells us that the earliest record of life at Masada is from the Hasmonean kings, a hundred years before Christ, who used the plateau as a sort of royal retreat. This sounds uncreative, but also unsurprising. I suppose the mighty have always felt the need to escape the riffraff, even before Queen Victoria built Buckingham Palace or Rupert Murdoch bought a jet. Privilege is not a new concept in human history.

As the bus pulls into the parking lot, I'm happy to see that the sky has cleared and is properly blue. Tourists like a blue sky, and today I'm a tourist in hiking shorts and shoes.

"Divide into groups," Rula says. "There's an introductory film, and then you take a cable car to the top. Once you get up there, the tour is mandatory, and the guides are provided by the site. The tour takes about an hour and a half. After that, you're on your own. You can stay as long as you choose. Just don't miss the last cable car down!"

Climbing off the air-conditioned bus, we're assaulted by the heat. It must be over 100 degrees. A steady wind blows the hot air straight into our faces.

"With this sun, it'll only get hotter, right?" Kyle says. "So let's go straight to the top and see the film later."

It makes sense. A group of us climbs aboard the cable car for the six-minute trip to the top. The car swings precariously, and the mechanism creaks. We clutch the handrails. I don't have any fear of heights, and still the ride is discombobulating. The steep walls of the plateau seem to cruise past our swinging toes. No wonder people chatter, plotting their descent even while we ascend. Someone noticed signs for ice cream in the gift shop below. I understand their urge to return to level ground, to air conditioning. It's unnatural to be dangling like a spider on a thread in a blast furnace.

We disembark into a blinding sun. I touch my temples to make sure I'm wearing my hat and sunglasses. Even with those, I'm still squinting. After our group gathers, a guide tells us the history of this place. King Herod — the one from the Christmas narrative — decided to use Masada as a fortress, so he built reinforcements. It flourished for a while, but not long. A group of Jewish rebels, or extremists — the Zealots — took possession of Masada during the Jewish Revolt around 70 CE.

Eventually the Romans retaliated by laying siege to Masada. They built a ramp up one side of the plateau, shovel by laborious shovel. I look over the edge of the plateau and imagine the drama. Did the Zealots peer down from their fortress and watch the Romans make their daily encroachment? Did they grow hungrier and thirstier each day? The story goes that when the Romans finally breached the wall, they found that all the Zealots — some 900 people — had committed mass suicide rather than be taken.

"For this reason," our guide emphasizes, "Masada has become a powerful symbol of determination, heroism, and freedom."

The sun is so strong that I can believe this story. This is a place where death seems inevitable. Why not engage it head-on instead of letting it hunt you down?

We trudge from ruin to ruin while the guide explains what the various buildings were used for over the centuries. In Herod's time there were palaces. Residences. Kitchens. Storerooms. Bathhouses. Saunas. This last is so bizarre that I laugh aloud into the dry heat. Did she say "sauna"?

Someone asks the obvious question. "Where would they get water?"

"Water came up by donkey," the guide answers. "A caravan from the oasis below."

"That must have been some caravan," someone says.

"It was endless. Imagine a giant loop."

I look over the edge and, instead of picturing Romans with shovels, picture donkeys wending their way, nose to tail. The guide is explaining how the water was heated by solar power, but I'm still picturing the donkey caravan switchbacking up the trail. I suppose some slave had to unload each beast's precious cargo. I suppose the donkeys didn't get to drink the water they carried — it was too valuable. Yes, the life-giving water had been hauled under duress simply so it could be heated by the desert sun and steamed away into the thirsty air for some fat king's moment of pleasure!

When the tour is done, I mosey along and read the helpful interpretive plaques, hoping to find some bit of information, some scientific fact, some Bermuda Triangle-type hypothesis that would explain why this place is the locus of so much excess. Instead, the plaques say that the clues unearthed by archaeologists don't support the most dramatic stories. For instance, that cache of bones from a mass suicide of 900? It's nowhere to be found. Instead, a more modest but verifiable number might be thirty. Maybe it's comforting to realize that truth is elusive, that history collides with legend everywhere in this Holy Land. I think about that as I plop down in the shade of a massive rock.

A desert vista spreads before me, crumbly and colorless. The silence is vast. In the far distance is a shimmer, the Dead Sea in a bowl of whitened hills. As the sun climbs, the shade grows smaller and smaller until it is gone. I think of Psalm 121, one of the Pilgrim Psalms: "The sun shall not strike you by day, nor the moon by night." Was that just a preacher or poet's hyperbole? Or had the Psalmist never sat in this particular patch of desert where there is no reprieve? Maybe everyone needs to experience a place like this, where the sun is inescapable, the world enormous, and a human being so small. This place thins out the veil between human and divine — you can feel it. This is a sacred spot even if there's no shrine, no candles to buy and light. Perhaps the lack of human meddling makes this plateau seem even more sacred. I cup my hands around my sunglasses and peer through slitted eyes at the ruins encircling me, imagining the events these remnants once witnessed.

In the distance I hear a loud sound like public-address static. It occurs every twenty minutes or so as the cable-car deposits another load of tourists, and a microphone announces the car's imminent return trip. My watch says that this is the last call before my bus's departure. I get up and brush sand from the seat of my shorts. I'm a little sorry I stayed so long, even if it wasn't long enough. Not only did I miss my chance to see the film and soak in some air conditioning; I feel off-balance from being immersed in such stretching silence.

The cable car is full. With our arms raised over our heads to grasp the swinging straps, we're packed body to body. Body to stinky body. We cast our eyes discreetly down, the way people do on subways, waiting for the trip to end. About three-quarters of the way down the steep incline, the cable car comes to a lurching halt. Inside, a chorus of exclamations erupts in every language. We are suspended over a gorge, swinging. Camera Michael attempts to shoot some footage of shocked faces, but it's too crowded for him to use the viewfinder. Undaunted, he lifts the video camera above his head and points down. Like him, I want to document the drama of the moment. I want to record this taste of terror before it evaporates into the desert air.

I look around at faces. Most are strangers, but I spot a couple of my documentary teammates. Michael catches my eye and winks. He's good at finding humor in situations. Ashley's eyes are huge. Her mouth is working as if she wants to spout words too awful to utter. She's sweating, but we're all sweating — we've been sweating all day.

What a terrible experience this must be for someone with claustrophobia. Yet I can't help but feel elated. The feeling is irrational, of course. Something awful, something irrecoverable might happen. Yet I love this feeling of not knowing, of waiting for the deity to make up its mind about what to do with us.

Each minute stretches. The ride that was supposed to take six minutes stretches to twelve, then to eighteen. The mechanism makes creaking sounds that we can't interpret. Occasionally there's a jerk, followed by a sliding movement as the car slips along the cable. I realize that the cable might give way altogether, and I imagine that we will drop to our death.

Lord, my daughters! Watch over them!

My prayer is instant, going straight from my heart without pausing in my brain.

The cable car swings, and through the windows the distant desert floor appears, disappears, reappears. Everything about this experience heightens the sense that we're suspended between heaven and earth — indeed, the sense that anything might happen. When the engine does finally make the right kind of noises, where things catch and turn, the car slides one final time before resuming its normal descent. That final crazy bout of swinging seems to be an answer to my prayer.

When we finally step off the cable car, we each have some words on our lips to describe the ordeal to the onlookers.

"Oh, my God! Oh, my God!" exclaims Ashley. "And I'm not taking the Lord's name in vain — Oh, my God!" Jessica rushes to Ashley's side, and they clutch each other.

I know it was terrible, but to me there's something invigorating about terror, about scraping against the face of God and surviving. I feel like a child after a particularly scary roller coaster ride. Knowing that everything comes out all right, wouldn't I do it again?

After Masada, the bus takes us to the Dead Sea, which sits in a basin of hills striped white and gray with minerals. The Dead Sea is the lowest point on the surface of the earth and one of the planet's saltiest bodies of water, too salty to support animal life — hence its name. Even if we can't actually swim, we're ready to immerse ourselves in water. We go to one of the resorts on the sloping edge of the sea. The resort has a few clusters of palm trees and a central pool with a single lackluster fountain. We are each dispensed a plastic bag containing a dry roll slit open and laid with a thin piece of pink meat, a whole unpickled pickle, and an unripe piece of fruit that we cannot identify, something similar to an apricot. It doesn't take us long to eat a few bites and pronounce ourselves done.

We women take our swimsuits into a changing room. The mirrors are shiny pieces of metal, so at least we can't fuss too much about how we look. We come out wrapped in our towels and conscious of the cameras. We wobble down a path of rounded rocks to the water's edge. The rocks are smooth, but they're the size you want to palm, not step on.

The water itself is very clear, even though the shoreline is crusty white. The bigger rocks are frosted with stalagmites of salt. I pick up a wet rock and put my lips against it, tentatively, tasting the salt. The water splashing my toes is surprisingly warm. My feet are blistered, and the salt stings wherever the skin is broken. JoAnne says the salt is healing, and I want to believe her. I want to believe that pain can be healing.

We hobble further in, exclaiming, until the water is around our waists. We've been warned not to splash and to keep our faces away from the water.

Shane must have slipped — I didn't see it happen — and gets submerged in the water. He comes up raking at his face.

"There's a water spigot," yells Brian. "See it?"

Shane can't see it, of course, but someone on the shore helps him stumble over to it and get his face rinsed off. I wince, just watching. I don't blame him for not getting back in the water after that.

"Remember what they said," Jessica reminds us. "When it's deep enough, just sit." We sit back as if we're on chairs, except there are no chairs; there's only the salt of the sea, which buoys us up. We laugh. Charlie pulls his toes up in front of him.

"Is this like walking on water?" he asks. "Toes on water."

Emboldened, the rest of us pull our feet up. We bob like weighted yellow ducks.

"Now that's a view you don't see every day," says Michael. "Faces and toes but no bodies."

On the shore, the cameras roll. We know we look silly, like every other group of tourists. Nothing about it feels real.

I feel thirsty. How odd to be suspended in water that cannot slake thirst, that cannot sustain life.

Flotilla

Where do you get that living water?

IN THE BIBLE, Jesus is forever traipsing from town to town. I imagine him walking down dusty roads wearing sandals that don't have good arch support. It must have been very wearisome. No wonder he needed to stop and get water from a well. No wonder he asked that Samaritan woman for a drink. I always thought he asked as a lead-in to their conversation. He knew she was thirsty — not physically, but metaphorically — for living water, for salvation. Now I see that maybe Jesus wasn't only opening a conversation. Maybe he was actually thirsty. Traveling is hot, hard work. I'm feeling travel-weary from sitting on an air-conditioned bus with a water bottle!

We're headed north now, to "the Galilee," where we'll spend a few days. Stephen always adds the definite article — "the Galilee" — short, I suppose, for "the Galilee region." JoAnne picked up on that and has been adding "the" in front of random proper nouns to make me laugh. "Shall we go listen to the Stephen?" Sometimes it's fun to make jokes that have nothing to do with God or Jesus or the Bible.

We packed our bags for three nights, and were asked to include our swimsuits and a flashlight. On the bus JoAnne comments,

"I've been checking the moon, and it's been getting bigger every night. Maybe we'll go swimming under a full moon." It hadn't occurred to me to even hope. Somehow I assumed that the Sea of Galilee would be polluted, or that there would be a war raging across it, or that it would be surrounded by wire. I know that the Golan Heights, which is Israeli-occupied, borders the east side of the lake, and I'm not sure exactly how that works.

To break up the trip, the bus first takes us west to Caesarea Maritima, on the shore of the Mediterranean Sea, so we can see some pristine ruins. The day is picture-perfect, with a bright blue sky and the sun sparkling on turquoise water. The first ruins we pass belong to an aqueduct, and they run for miles.

Excavation is underway everywhere. Caesarea Maritima was a harbor city built by Herod about a generation before Jesus was born. The city's capstone was a pleasure palace built on a piece of real estate jutting out into the water. An amphitheater we tour is huge and stunning. I picture it filled with wildly cheering Roman citizens as the chariots race in long loops. What joy!

"Herod built this for races," says the guide, "but after the Jewish revolt of 70 CE, it was used for gladiator games. Some twenty-five hundred Jews were killed here." The gaily colored scene in my imagination ends abruptly.

The guide leads us through a maze of ruins to a particular wall. Like the other walls here, this one is constructed of cut stone. A series of partitions, or projections, extend from this wall like a rib cage.

"What do you think this area was used for?" the guide asks.

"Stalls for horses." "A dressing room." "Storage areas." Our guide is bemused and encourages us to keep guessing. People call out things we've seen in ruins elsewhere, no matter how unlikely they are here: "An olive press." "A bathhouse." "An altar."

"You're trying too hard," the guide tells us. "It's something a crowd would need, especially in a venue of this size."

"A restroom?" someone asks.

"That's right. A toilet. Multiple toilets, actually."

Michael and Charlie immediately climb onto the stone projections to take a seat. They make funny faces as they try to situate themselves with a cheek on each stone projection.

"Maybe they had bigger butts back then," JoAnne suggests.

"You stand on the stones," says the guide. "They're for squatting, not sitting."

While the guys mimic squatting, to everyone's merriment, the guide points out two grooves near the bottom of the stone wall. "These are troughs. Fresh water would be continuously pumped during events, one trough for constant flushing and one for hand-washing."

"Four people at a time — pretty neat! Better than some concerts I've been to," says Ashley.

"But what about being smack-dab next to each other like that?" one of the older women asks.

"I wouldn't mind sharing," says JoAnne. "After all, everybody poops."

"That's your whole theology, isn't it!" exclaims Charlie.

"Well, it's true," says JoAnne.

☂ ☂ ☂

We get back in the bus to ride another two hours or so, east toward the Sea of Galilee. We arrive at our lodgings just before suppertime. Pilgerhaus is a large facility sprawled along the western shoreline of the Sea of Galilee. There are multiple buildings and beautiful landscaping.

I've heard Bible place names all my life: Bethlehem, Jerusalem, Nazareth, Galilee. One of the gifts of this pilgrimage is the very different mental pictures I will attach to each of those names from now on. Today I realize that the Galilee region, where Jesus grew up, is much more verdant than Jerusalem. There's color everywhere: green and yellow grass, pink and purple flowers, trees dripping red blossoms. Not only is there more color, but the light isn't as harsh. Perhaps in Jerusalem all the rock and sand reflect the desert sun.

Our rooms are surprisingly modern, with ceramic tile and

modular beds. JoAnne and I exclaim over our new digs and take luxurious showers. When we walk into the dining room, we're greeted by a man in his thirties who clasps both of JoAnne's hands, then both of mine.

"My name is Victor, and what a lucky man I am! I am a Palestinian, and I have a job! What's more, I have a job serving food to beautiful women such as yourselves!"

I decide to let myself be susceptible to his charms. Isn't that part of the allure of travel?

We sit down to a well-appointed table. There are the local foods we have come to expect — pita bread and salads and lamb and eggplant — but more besides. I eat my fill of broiled fish and fresh green beans swimming in butter. We buy wine from Victor, then clink our glasses to this new chapter of our pilgrimage. The wine is called Cremisan, and it's made by Palestinians on their ancient lands. We solemnly toast our solidarity with them — and each other.

After dinner we decide to change into our suits and go for a swim. It's mainly the documentary group plus a few others, including Krisha, the young woman who's hoping to see Jesus on the shore of the Sea of Galilee. We pick our way, barefoot, to the rocky lakeshore and understand why we were told to bring flashlights. They aren't necessary tonight, though, because the moon is full and bright.

Brian and Camera Michael, our full-service filmmakers, had stopped earlier to buy inflatable inner tubes. The first pilgrims in the water call encouragingly to the rest of us. Their happy voices carry across the water. The rocks on the shoreline are the size of chicken eggs and make for slow going. I'm a bit afraid I'll turn an ankle. And I know I'll need my pilgrim feet tomorrow.

The water is soft and warm. Just yesterday the salt water of the Dead Sea stung the blisters of my feet, but this is an entirely different experience. This water is soothing, with a texture like silk. It must be chock-full of minerals. I have the sensation that I'm slipping into a second skin, an undergarment. The skin of my feet is already plumping in this water. My calves and thighs drink it in. I walk deeper, to my waist and beyond. I'm buoyant as I breast-stroke. I've never felt more graceful in water. I feel elevated by the very touch of it.

I'm not the only one whose spirits are rising. The day of too much bus exhaust is becoming a dim memory. Our group gets sillier as the moments pass. We start splashing. I can tell that dunking is only moments away. I put my whole head in the water so I won't have to fear it. Besides, I want to coat my hair with this wonderful elixir.

"Jesus swam in this very lake," Ashley says.

"In this very same water," someone echoes.

"It would be different water," someone else says, correctively, and a science debate ensues. The water would have evaporated and rained down a million times between then and now. Yes, but a lot of that water would have stayed in this same region. And what about the minerals? I listen with one ear, enjoying the silliness. I decide to believe that this is the very same water that Jesus stepped in, that some critical mass of the substance of the water is the same. Sometimes theology is like that: you listen, you think, and in the end you choose what you want to believe.

I dive and swim underwater, the water encasing me like a glove. The possibility that this very same water encased the body of Jesus is almost too much glory to bear. I feel emotions similar to those I felt at the Stone of Anointing, only now the divine presence is tinged with joy rather than sorrow. Jesus' body lay on that slab in death, but this water encased his body in life, in the throes of life, while he helped with the fishing nets or cooled off from a dusty day of walking.

Someone brings the leftover dinner wine down to the lake. We don't have glasses, so we pass the bottles from hand to hand. We've all tasted better wine than this Cremisan, but nothing can be more delicious than this night. Nothing can be better than this Palestinian wine, as we drink it under a Palestinian moon, honoring Jesus.

We lean back, floating and enjoying the Sea of Galilee. The moon is a round disc, shining through the clouds and painting a shimmering path on the water. I imagine that it beckoned the ancient people as it beckons me. What did that path of light say to Jesus when he went night fishing with his disciples? Did it speak to him of peace? Above us on a high plateau, the lights of the Golan Heights wink and flicker. I understood, before, that the Golan Heights has been a political football between Syria and Israel, but seeing how high this land towers, and also its proximity to water, I can understand better why the nations fight.

At the very moment that I'm glimpsing Jesus as the Prince of Peace, I'm also glimpsing the strategic importance of the Golan Heights. So it goes in this Holy Land.

JoAnne and I grasp the same bottle of wine so that we can lie back and float and keep the bottle of wine upright between us. Ashley hooks on to the bottle, and then Kyle. We make a four-armed starfish. It occurs to me that I must be drunk to feel like this, but I'm not. More pilgrims float by, another starfish.

"Everybody!" someone yells. "Let's all float altogether."

We link up by fingers and toes, by ankles and shins and wrists.

"Now!" We make a flotilla, a giant starfish, a star. We become one organism. We last only a moment before the first person starts to sink, and the whole flotilla goes down. We try again, lasting a bit longer. We try counting before we begin. It helps to start at the exact same moment. The biggest problem is the laughing. We simply can't stop. Our joy is buoyant and inescapable.

Each time there's a countdown, I lean back to float. With my eyes open and my ears submerged, the laughing of my friends recedes. It's like entering a great solitude, even while in the company of a great many saints. When I'm submerged, everything is blotted out except this body of water and this night sky. I've never seen stars this bright from my home in the suburbs of Washington, D.C. Even on the rooftop in Jerusalem, the stars weren't this crisp.

I close my eyes and listen underwater but hear only the very distant sound of laughter. I think about the water that's stopping my ears, the same water that Peter and Andrew and James and John caught fish in, and I'm so overcome that I can hardly breathe. I immediately begin to sink and must stand up with a great splash.

All around is hilarity. We're brushing against something ineffable, some presence that lingers in this water and this moon, some presence that makes us so happy that we must do something. Charlie is in one of the inner tubes. He fills an empty wine bottle with the water of Galilee and pours it over his head. He yells, "Y'all need to get freed up!" He refills the bottle and empties it again. "Get freed up!" He is baptizing himself with this delicious Galilean water. I hope it gives him exactly what he needs. Every pilgrim needs a supply of living water.

❦   ❦   ❦

At breakfast I fill my plate at the buffet. Victor visits my table. "How was your swim last night?"

"You know we went swimming?" I ask.

He laughs. "Who could sleep with the shouting and laughing all night?"

I feel chagrined. I'd forgotten how sound carries across water. "I'm so sorry if we bothered you," I say.

Victor laughs again, heartily. "Bother? Bother is rocket missiles. Bother is not laughter! Go ahead — be crazy! It's the only way to be in this crazy war. Today we are lucky to be alive!"

CHAPTER 15

Multiply

How many loaves have you? Go and see.

MARK 6:38

TABGHA IS THE place where Jesus miraculously fed a crowd
of five thousand people with only five small loaves of bread
and two fish, which generated twelve baskets of leftovers. Maybe
it's because JoAnne and I have been sharing a dorm room named
Tabgha, but I've been dreaming about those loaves. The story is
familiar. It's told in all four Gospels — plus, as if for good measure, Matthew and Mark include a second version where Jesus
feeds four thousand people. This miraculous feeding is obviously
a pivotal story.

Some preachers turn this text into a type of Sesame Street
parable about sharing. When the boy shared his lunch, so did
everyone else, and then there was enough — so we should share.
Well, yes, we should share, but is that the point? Was the lunch
that day simply the miracle of potluck?

Other preachers go the symbolic route. This shared meal was a
feast in the manner of Holy Communion, a high and holy ritual
rather than actual nourishment. Each person pinched off a tiny
crumb of bread and proclaimed it satisfying. Well, yes, communion is satisfying, but is that the point? What about those five
thousand hungry people?

I understand why people pick a particular interpretation. It's a way of making the text manageable. We like to understand things, and the easiest way to understand Scripture is to reduce it to one simple point. More important, perhaps, is figuring out the central question and whether or not we can answer it satisfactorily. Is this Tabgha story about the human need to consume something? Does it ask us what we hunger for? Or does it ask us to ponder abundance?

Even children understand these questions. I remember a time I taught this lesson in Sunday school. I drew stick figures on paper, photocopied them to equal a crowd of five thousand, then taped the figures all around the room so the children could imagine being in a crowd that size, and hungry. What would it take to feed us all? The children's eyes grew large as they looked around, and one child said, "Jesus always has enough."

🐟 🐟 🐟

The bus pulls up. It's perfect. There's an expanse of rocks and grass leading down to the Sea of Galilee. You can immediately picture how a crowd could gather and see without obstruction. The water would provide a sort of natural megaphone from behind Jesus. After last night's experience, with the sound of our joy traveling across the water, I'm unlikely to forget that detail.

There's a sizable courtyard and gift shop, but the shrine itself is a simple stone church. I like it immediately because of its clean lines. Intersecting stone archways create a domed roof. There are only a few pews, exceedingly plain — what Ikea would make if Ikea made pews. The eye is drawn to a stunning piece of black ironwork that hangs over the stone altar. The altar was constructed over the rock where Jesus placed the loaves and fishes when he blessed them. In front of the altar is a mosaic depicting a fish on either side of a bowl holding bread rolls. Tradition says that Jesus stood exactly where this mosaic was laid.

Under the altar is the sacred rock itself, which you may kneel down and touch. It would be easy to scoff at the authenticity of this rock, to wonder if it is the actual rock where Jesus laid the bread and fish. Who would remember exactly which rock Jesus used in a field of rocks? How would that knowledge have been passed from generation to generation — at least with any kind of verifiability? Nobody used surveying equipment to mark the spot, did they? And even if it's the actual rock, wasn't it just a random rock, handily flat and conveniently located? Was there anything sacred about that rock?

I kneel to examine this "rock of multiplication." It's broad and bumpy, and blackened from the touch of so many human hands. So many humans needing so many things multiplied. A simple oil lamp is perched in one crevice. Tightly rolled papers are tucked in other crevices. Bits of paper are scattered about, like the fortunes from broken cookies. I look at all these slips of paper, all these human needs, and wonder about the people who left them on this rock. What needed to be multiplied in their lives?

And what about me — what do I need multiplied? I cannot decide because I have plenty of everything. I have people to love and work to do. To ask for more while on a trip like this would seem downright greedy. I decide to write a simple prayer — for abundance. After all, I'm in the place where God showed great abundance. A boy gave Jesus his lunch, and abundance flowed to the crowd. I study the mosaic — those two fish and five loaves — and realize what a nice lunch the boy gave up.

It strikes me that, before there could be abundance, the boy had to give up what he already had. Why have I never realized this?

But I haven't. I haven't asked myself what I might need to give up in order for it to be multiplied. What do I have in adequate amount for myself that I desire to have in greater abundance to share with others? As I crouch beside the rock, the answer is obvious: words, written words. I live out my call to ministry through writing: sermons, fiction, nonfiction. How would my life change if I gave my words to Jesus and he blessed them? I fear that the world will laugh at my words, at their inadequacy, so I fret over them. I have trouble releasing them to the world. Squatting there, I realize that I have never given my written words, without reservation, to Jesus. I want to do that. I want to write down my intention and leave it as a sort of promissory note to Jesus: I give you my words.

As I'm scribbling this onto a page, an announcement comes over the loudspeaker: The tour bus is loading. I tear the prayer from my journal, roll it tightly, and leave it on the rock.

Running across the courtyard, I notice that JoAnne is in the gift shop, pawing madly through a rack of T-shirts. The shirts have a picture of the Tabgha mosaic across the chest, and I understand instantly why she wants one. I want one, too. I want a reminder of miraculous multiplication. We each grab a shirt and hurry to the cash register.

"What are we trying to buy, anyway?" I ask her, panting a bit.

"A souvenir," she says. "Of abundance."

Yes. As a remembrance of God's willingness to give us abundance without limit or price tag, we each plunk down a credit card to buy a Hanes Beefy-T.

Pilgrims with plastic.

CHAPTER 16

Cheek to Cheek

Ephphatha! Be opened!

MARK 7:34

"WHEN THESE PEOPLE read about the miracle at Cana, they're reading about their neighbors," JoAnne says to everyone on the bus. "Imagine that."

We're headed to Reine, the town just down the road from Cana, where Jesus performed his first miracle. He turned water into wine at a wedding reception because his mother asked him to.

"Do you think they do a lot of weddings?" asks Michael.

"Maybe wedding receptions," says Charlie. "Fun ones, with lots of wine — not like ours!"

We will worship at the Church of the Holy Family in Reine on this Sunday morning. Other than the fact that this church is just down the road from Cana in Galilee — and that it's been there for some two thousand years — worshiping at Reine feels surprisingly similar to worshiping in my Presbyterian church in suburban D.C. One similarity is that the congregations are about the same size. In a word: small. When the forty of us pilgrims enter the sanctuary at Holy Family, we roughly double the number of worshipers. Another similarity is the size of the church building. Holy Family is a few hundred years old, built of rough-cut stone. My church is 140 years old, built of brick. Even the two organs sound the same. This organ, like the one back home, has a tendency to sound a bit like a roller-rink Wurlitzer, especially if the organist gets carried away and begins to rollick. Here's a difference in the churches: this church has a stained-glass window showing the Holy Family. Hardly surprising, except that Mary and Joseph and the boy Jesus all have blond hair and blue eyes.

The priest, Father Samuel Barhoum, preaches on the healing of the deaf man who is also mute. The brief text is from Mark 7, a straightforward miracle of Jesus. Father Barhoum preaches first in Arabic, then in English. I love hearing the command in Aramaic: *Ephphatha!* (EP-fa-tha). The phrase is a tongue twister, which is a bit ironic, given its meaning: Be opened! Open your ears! Your eyes! Your mouth!

Father Barhoum asks, "How long has it been since you talked with another person with a truly open heart, not judging anything about them? How long since you listened to the Spirit of God rather than culture or your own desires? How long since you opened yourself to God's will, rather than obsessing over your own?"

I feel convicted by the simplicity and power of the message. It's no easy thing to be open. That's why pilgrimage is so challenging. It's easier to protect my belief system than to open it for scrutiny. But how can it be useful if it's closed? Even a treasure chest needs to be open. I try to absorb this sermon as God's word to me today.

But the preacher isn't done. He turns to us pilgrims and asks us, point-blank, to be ambassadors for the Christians of the Holy Land. "We need your solidarity," he says. "We need your support. We need you to open your eyes and see our situation. We need you to open your ears to hear our pain. We need you to open your tongue to tell others. For we are the living stones, and we will not die. But these are hard times, and we need your help."

Since my childhood days, I've known that "living stones" refers to people who make up the church — not physically, in the way that stones construct a building, but spiritually. In Sunday school we had a song with hand motions: "I am the church. You are the church. We are the church together!" But now, after spending just a handful of days in Israel and Palestine, it is time to see living stones with grownup eyes. On the one hand, we are surrounded by buildings constructed of gorgeous stone hewn from this holy ground, which seems poignant and powerful. Yet, because of politics and religious rivalry, the church work is handicapped, and Christians are encouraged — both directly and obliquely — to leave this Holy Land. If that happens, the beautiful stone buildings that remain will be nothing more than dead stones, a memorial to what was once alive.

After Father Barhoum's Amen, the congregation sings the Lord's Prayer in Arabic. My heart wells up. What do I know of their experience, really? I happen to be sitting in a pew beside an aged grandmother. Her cheek can barely contain all the wrinkles that crisscross each other. On the other side of the grandmother is a woman who sings the prayer with absolute conviction, as if she has sung it countless times and believes every word. She's holding a young girl on her lap. The singer reminds me of a member of my congregation who sings the same way. The young girl reminds me of myself, growing up. I always felt so at home in church. I used to sit snuggled against my mother with my arm linked through hers while the minister preached. Does this young girl feel the same connection to her mother? I smile at her, my sister, as she sings in Arabic and I sing in English.

It's time for communion. After extending the invitation to the table, the priest gives the words of peace and asks us to share the peace with one another. I sit down beside the grandmother so I can more comfortably grasp her hand and say "Salaam." She leans forward and wobbles her cane next to me. Wordlessly, she leans her face against mine, cheek to cheek. Despite the maze of wrinkles, her cheek is as soft as cashmere. I remember my own grandmothers, long gone, and the elderly women I have been pastor to. I love the wisdom etched in wrinkles. They are testimony to both sorrow and joy, which feel so permanent but pass. While I'm thinking these things, the grandmother turns her face to me and kisses me full on the lips. I feel as if some saint has descended to confer a blessing. Fresh tears spring to my eyes as she pats my knee. It's time to pass the peace to others. I blink and shake hands with the pilgrims on the other side of me, and behind me, and in front of me. We were strangers not ten days ago, and now we are each part of this Holy Family.

"Ephphatha! Be opened!" Jesus commands, and we must respond. He does not say, "Be opened if you feel that your personal history will allow you to be comfortable with that level of vulnerability." He simply commands us to "be open." The commands are not difficult to understand, but they are difficult to follow. I wonder how I might respond to this command, and what it will cost me. Should I become more politically involved with the people of Palestine? Should I risk finding an outlet for my writing, an audience beyond the congregation I preach to each Sunday? It's easier to stay trapped behind my eyes, seeing what I have always seen.

I get in line to receive communion, letting the priest lay the wafer in my hand so I can slip it on my tongue, then take a sip from the common cup. The organist begins the closing hymn, which is deeply familiar, even though I haven't sung it in decades. The congregation sings in Arabic, which makes it challenging for my memory to match words to tune, but eventually I do. It's a child's hymn from my Sunday school days called "How Shall the Young Direct Their Way?":

> *Sincerely I have sought Thee, Lord,*
> *O let me not from Thee depart;*
> *To know Thy will and keep from sin,*
> *Thy Word I cherish in my heart.*

Singing these words, I am reminded: This is the rock from which I am hewn, this Reformed faith with its emphasis on the Word of God, and on knowing the will of God, and on keeping from sin. Yes, there are some good things about this familiar rock!

🌿 🌿 🌿

After the worship service, there is coffee hour — just like back home. We're served scalding Turkish coffee in miniature plastic cups. I can manage to hold mine only by the rim. It's both challenge and delight to get the thick brew down. Plus, there are trays of pastries with various fillings, including my favorite, poppy seed.

After we're given some time to mingle with the members of the congregation, we have the chance to hear Father Barhoum's wife, Susan, tell her story. The first thing Susan says is that she can trace her family tree to the fourth century. Every branch of that tree is Christian. In fact, her family has been Christian since the time of Jesus.

I try to digest this, wondering how many centuries of my family have been Christian. Maybe too many to count — though we wouldn't count generations since Jesus, as Susan does. We'd perhaps count from John Calvin, some five hundred years ago. Or from Abraham Kuyper, who was credited with the birth of neo-Calvinism in the Netherlands just over a hundred years ago. How would it change things if we counted from Jesus instead?

Are the Reformers, with their complicated histories, even the right heritage to claim? Should we, for example, claim John Calvin, who labeled Michael Servetus a heretic for rejecting the doctrine of the Trinity and who supported the latter's burning at the stake? Kuyper was an intellectual giant, but his views were claimed as support by the Afrikaner Broederbond in South Africa, which in turn shaped the great evil of apartheid. At the same time, Reformed church members in the Netherlands sheltered Jews from the Nazis. Religion is complicated stuff, peopled by tragically flawed humans who are, nevertheless, capable of great courage and theological insight. I can't claim just my favorite pieces of this history. I have to claim it all.

Susan's family members were displaced from their home by Israeli soldiers and put in refugee camps. They never returned to the family home, though her grandfather carried the key to that house for the rest of his life. She shows emotion as she shares these powerful stories of past suffering. Yet her passion intensifies as she describes her current work. She pours her energy into various peace initiatives for businesspersons and for children.

How powerfully our religious history shapes us. Yet it can shape us in different ways. We choose our response. Susan could have become bitter and let the painful history of the Palestinian Christians poison her; instead, she chooses to follow Jesus in the way of peace. Her story challenges me to learn more about my own religious history. Before I came on this pilgrimage, I thought I was done exploring my faith history and was concerned only with the future, bright and shiny, but now I see that the past is never gone, that it becomes the seedbed for whatever new thing might spring up.

CHAPTER 17

Transform

We ourselves heard this voice come from heaven while we were
with him on the holy mountain.

2 PETER 1:18

MOUNT TABOR IS easily visible from a distance. The
mountain rises abruptly from a flat plain, as conical as a
breast. Stephen tells us that pilgrims often spend hours hiking
up the steep mountain. We won't, of course. We may be pilgrims,
but we're doing pilgrimage North American-style — in comfort
and in a hurry. Our itinerary allots a half-day for this mountain
and its glory.

Our bus arrives at the foot of the mountain, and we must
switch to taxis because the road becomes a series of hairpin turns,
the angles too acute for a bus. I climb into the back seat of a cab
between two friends. We're wedged tight, but, as it turns out, not
tight enough. The taxi charges up the incline and, as it takes the
first turn, throws the lot of us against the left side of the taxi. As
the taxi doubles back, we squash to the right side. Then left. Then
right. The windows are open to the rushing wind. The mountain
drops away just beyond the apex of each turn.

"You wanna get high?" Michael yells from the front seat.

We zigzag up the mountain, careening back and forth across
the seat. When a taxi passes in the opposite direction, the drivers
yell to each other out their open windows. We laugh at the same

time that we cry out and hang on. Maybe distress and delight are not so far apart. Wasn't that the lesson of the cable car?

At the top we emerge from the cab, breathless and rumpled, into a serene garden. A wide gravel path is bordered with trees and flowering shrubs, and worn by the footsteps of thousands of pilgrims. The path leads to the Church of the Transfiguration, sitting on the mountain's tip-top. The basilica was built over the very rock where Jesus was transfigured. Our group gradually gathers as taxi-loads of pilgrims arrive.

The Transfiguration story is one of those dramatic narratives that feels slippery, like there's some vital point we humans miss. Jesus took a select few of his disciples — Peter and James and John — to this mountaintop and became radiant like the sun, his clothes whiter than any bleach on earth could make them. The long-deceased prophets Moses and Elijah materialized on either side of Jesus, also dressed in dazzling white.* Imagine what that was like for the plain-clothed disciples.

On this day the view of the valley is hazy and tinged with blue. Stephen tells us about the imposing stone basilica we can see behind his shoulder, and I jot down the facts: "Church built in three sections in the Roman style in 1924. . . ."

Kyle whispers to me, "Are you still being so compulsive?"

"What? This is sermon fodder."

"You're telling me you visit this mountaintop" — he gestures expansively to the vista — "where Jesus shone like the sun, and your people want to hear" — he glances at my notes — "'Roman style, 1924'?"

"Maybe I like facts."

"No doubt." Kyle's Canadian accent gives both vowels their due even as he laughs. "Facts are easy. Pilgrimage is hard." He taps my still-open page. "Go ahead. Write that down."

I snap my journal shut. I know he's right. We're not here for facts. We're here to be pilgrims, to move from one place with God to another place with God. I don't know where my pilgrim path

---

*Compare the Transfiguration accounts in Matthew 17:1-8, Mark 9:2-8, and Luke 9:28-36.

leads, exactly, but I suspect it will be somewhere I'm afraid to go. Yet I do want to arrive at a wider world. I prefer this pilgrim way over the constrained way I grew up. This more spacious pilgrim way leads to a mountaintop — literally, but also metaphorically. I'm having glimpses of the kingdom of God, moments when my heart overflows with love. This isn't just an idea. It's not a thought process or a doctrinal position; it's trying to see with the eyes of Christ. It's the cells in my body knowing I'm connected to every other person on the planet. Not just because we share biology, or the Internet, but because we share grace. We come from the same Creator and someday will return to that One. And in between we share the same Spirit. These are notions that belong to mountaintops, where the veil between heaven and earth lifts.

We're still standing in front of the Church of the Transfiguration, and now I've missed most of Stephen's facts about this building. But why is there a building on this mountaintop at all? Scripture records that Peter, ever hopeful, ever awkward, offered to build booths for the three resplendent beings who shimmered before him, a suggestion that hung in the air until it was brushed away for the irrelevant comment it was. You can't nail down glory, Peter!

But later crews of workers attempted to do just that, of course. They built a stone church in three parts: a central nave to honor Jesus, with a chapel on either side, one for Moses and one for Elijah. We're told that there's a stunning central mosaic, and each prophet has his own mural depicting a mountaintop moment.

"There's a trapdoor in the floor of the nave," says Stephen, "and underneath that door is the bedrock of the mountain. People leave prayers there. You get fifteen minutes."

The central mosaic is indeed gorgeous, sparkling in gold. It shows Jesus in shining raiment, flanked by the prophets, with the disciples looking awestruck. I take this in, then step into the side chapels. I catalog each mural rather than experience it, the way you do when you've been in too many museums but know you may never return to this one. You want to be able to say, "I saw that." Moses' mural shows him receiving the Tablets of

the Law on Mount Sinai. Elijah's mural shows him on top of
Mount Carmel, managing the cosmic duel between the God of
the Israelites, Yahweh, and the Canaanite god Baal.

I notice the other pilgrims investigating the chapels, but I
don't want to take the time. I'm mainly interested in the bedrock.
I hurry to the open trapdoor and peek inside. Scraps of paper
litter the rock. I glimpse words in many languages, very few in
English. Still, some words jump out at me, and I comprehend
their meaning: "illumine," "capacity," "adore." I want to join this
company of pilgrims and entrust my words to this rock. I take a
seat in the nave and write a prayer in my journal:

> *Yahweh, Transform me. The moments of glory are all around. May
> I have the eyes and heart to see them, then let them go, trusting
> they will come again. Open me.*

I write it out again and tear the scrap of paper from the binding.
I kneel and reach through the trapdoor to place the torn paper
on the rock. My fingertips graze the slips of paper laid by other
pilgrims, then touch the bedrock itself, rock that is smooth and
cold, rock that Jesus stepped on, rock that witnessed Christ's
glory when heaven opened. The contact, for a moment, is like
brushing up against a presence both ephemeral and eternal,
something beyond time.

So I stumble to a pew, instinctively realizing that in order to
hold onto this glory I must make room. I must leave something
behind. I must let go of the baggage I carry around with me, the
wounds, the resentments, the grudges. The only way I know how
to do that is to pray, so I pray for forgiveness, for myself and for
those who have wronged me. I repeat: *Open me, open me, open . . .*

Someone is tapping my shoulder. We pilgrims must leave. I
notice that Ashley is sitting on the floor, her face tear-streaked.
I wonder what's going on for her, but don't ask. This pilgrim
journey is hard to process, let alone share. We all need space.

The group of us walks back toward the spot where the taxis
will pick us up. We pass brown-robed Franciscan friars who live

on this mountaintop. Some are reading beneath flowering trees, haloed by pink and white. One monk plays a recorder and one a small harp; another stares into the middle distance. We call out "Shalom!" Each monk looks up and returns our greeting with a rapturous smile.

What do these monks know that we don't? Although we might wish we could reside on a mountaintop of glory, wouldn't we miss our lives, our actual lives down on the ground? Someday we will all live on a mountaintop, so to speak, in that juncture between heaven and earth, in the kingdom of God. But for now we must settle for the briefest encounter with the holy, a brushing cheek to cheek. I remember worshiping beside the grandmother in Reine, her wrinkled cheek against mine; swimming in the Sea of Galilee, the velvet water against my skin; praying beside the Jewish mother and her baby at the Western Wall, our cheeks against the ancient stone.

JoAnne and Kyle are chatting as we walk along. Kyle says, "The Transfiguration accounts are really similar in the different Gospels. I was comparing them last night."

"It's the timing that changes, isn't it?" JoAnne asks.

"They all use the word 'bleach,' don't they?" I add. "But did they have bleach back then?"

"I think they used urine," JoAnne says.

"Matthew doesn't say 'bleach,'" Kyle says.

"Maybe Matthew thought of a better word," I say. "Maybe Mark had already written it down, verbatim, so Peter got stuck with his bad choice of words."

"Peter and his words!" JoAnne exclaims. "Hey, let's build some booths!"

"That's what proves the dialogue is authentic," Kyle says. "Otherwise, you could think that Peter made the whole story up just to make himself look good."

"But he doesn't look good," JoAnne counters. "And I'm glad. You gotta love a disciple who says the wrong thing."

"I feel for him," I say. "Even more so after today. So he wanted to hang onto the moment of glory. Wouldn't you have?"

"Of course. Look at the documentary," says JoAnne. "What's Brian trying to capture with — "

She stops in her tracks, staring overhead into some low-hanging tree branches. "Aren't those peppercorns?"

Kyle reaches up and breaks off a twig and hands it to her. The sprig has a cluster of little pink balls, some plump and some withered. JoAnne inhales deeply, then smiles broadly at me and Kyle. "Now this is what will remind me of glory."

As we arrive where the taxis will pick us up, I remember something. "About those murals — did you get a good look at Moses? It proves something I've always wondered about."

"What's that?" Kyle asks.

I let a delicious moment pass before replying. "Did you notice? Moses really does look like Charlton Heston."

CHAPTER 18

Weep

Jerusalem, Jerusalem, the city that kills the prophets and stones those who are sent to it!

MATTHEW 23:37

THE TEN DAYS of our pilgrimage began with an introduction to Jerusalem, then roughly followed the chronology of Jesus' life as we traveled from Bethlehem to Galilee. Now we're back in Jerusalem to journey the final lap of Jesus' story.

Today we will explore the Mount of Olives, just outside the walls of Jerusalem. We begin in the courtyard of the chapel at Bethphage, where Jesus began his journey by donkey on Palm Sunday. Even though it's very early, the sun is already bright. We're all slouched under hats and sunglasses as if we could protect ourselves against the sun's rays. The air is intensely dry. Stephen begins to talk about Jesus' dual nature, human and divine. I'm tired of squinting while he lectures, but I'm ready to look anew at old questions.

Stephen says that each Gospel writer used a particular lens for Jesus, a way of answering Jesus' foundational question: *Who do you say that I am?* Stephen uses his sternest voice: "As we travel this Holy Week path, we must keep this question in the front of our minds. It is the essential question to the Palm Sunday story — and to every story this week. Who did the crowds think Jesus was? When we say 'Messiah,' what does that mean? A teacher to set them loose from religious law? A healer to cure their diseases? A liberator to free them from Roman rule?"

Someone reads aloud Mark's version of the Palm Sunday story (Mark 11:1-10). It is brief and familiar. The jubilant crowd waves palm branches as Jesus rides into Jerusalem on a donkey. They shout, "Hosanna! Blessed is the One who comes in the name of the Lord!" The simple story rings with innocent joy. Because of that, church leaders often delegate it to the children. Many times I have led little ones waving palm branches while the congregation sings "All Glory, Laud, and Honor."

I say to Ashley, "Have you led palm processionals?"

"Oh, brother," she answers. "How do you stop the kids from hitting each other with the branches?"

"I know it!"

"I guess it's human nature to turn holy things into weapons," she says. "But still."

Stephen is saying something about the chapel. "There's a fence around a stone that the Crusaders revered as the stone Jesus used to mount the donkey. Remember that riding a donkey is a sign of peace. Conquering war heroes rode horses."

The architecture of the chapel is simple enough: a rectangle constructed of stone. What's complicated are the interior frescoes, all life-sized. High on the front wall, Jesus rides a brown donkey while the people lay down colorful cloaks and green palm branches with contagious energy. On the other three walls, the figures waving palm branches are in less dramatic, sepia tones. I study individuals as though I'm people-watching in downtown D.C., noting this woman's expression, that man's head garb, this child's uncovered toes, that baby in a bundle. In one place in the fresco there's an opening that seems intentional, and I realize that this is where I can insert myself. I'm grateful to the artist. I want to slip into the adoring crowd. My pilgrim heart is full of devotion for this Jesus of Nazareth, the one I've been chasing for days. The one who's been chasing me for years.

"Blessed is the One who comes in the name of the Lord. Hosanna!"

We fill the pews to sing a few verses of "All Glory, Laud, and Honor." I don't have to worry about children fiddling with their palm branches inappropriately. Instead, with my eyes on Jesus, I can become one of the children — wrapped in a second innocence. I sit down to write a prayer:

> *Dear Lord, I come to you as a child. I dedicate myself to you, even though I know what lies ahead, as those children did not. I will be tested. But I adore you and never mean to stop. Amen.*

When the hymn is done, people wander off to examine the frescoes. Charlie, Jessica, and another pilgrim begin to sing "The Lord's Prayer," and I join them. We loop our arms across each other's shoulders, our heads together in a tight square. The acoustics are perfect; the sound rebounds just enough to gain depth. The words of the song — "Our Father" — are something we can each sing with complete abandon. Some other hymn, some other praise song, might reveal our theological differences, our various answers to Jesus' question: *Who do you say that I am?* But for this moment, as our voices blend and ascend from within the walls of this sanctuary, our prayer is as unified and fragrant as incense.

❦ ❦ ❦

The group gathers and walks up the long, sloping path of the Mount of Olives. There are two churches between this chapel at Bethphage and the Garden of Gethsemane, both rather recently built. The first is a small chapel called Dominus Flevit, and the second is the much larger Church of All Nations.

We gather outside Dominus Flevit (Latin for "the Lord wept"). Stephen has someone read Matthew 23:37: "Jerusalem, Jerusalem, the city that kills the prophets and stones those who are sent to it! How often have I desired to gather your children together as a hen gathers her brood under her wings, and you were not willing!" Jesus spoke these emotional words while standing in this spot overlooking Jerusalem, knowing that his death was inevitable. The chapel was built here to honor those poignant words, words that drip with sorrow. Jesus knew that the powers that occupied Jerusalem did not welcome him, either the Roman political power represented by Herod or the Jewish religious power represented by the Sanhedrin.

"Some interpret these words of Jesus as judgment," Stephen says. "You must decide that for yourself. What I can tell you for sure is that this chapel was built in the shape of a teardrop."

Then Stephen talks about tears. He reminds us that Scripture explicitly says that Jesus wept before he raised Lazarus from the dead. There is no parallel verse in Scripture saying that Jesus laughed, although we assume he did. When he wept, Jesus broke the cultural taboo against weeping.

"What freedom this gives us — what permission to cry!" Stephen leans forward. "Tears are central to the human story. Everybody is born crying. This life is a 'vale of tears,' and when we die, others weep for us."

I look at my feet as he talks. My own cheeks are once again wet with tears. You'd hardly think that could happen in the dry air of this Holy Land, but I've had wet cheeks every day of this pilgrimage. At first I thought my tears were evidence of my unworthiness, but now I've come to see them differently. They evidence my passion as I wrestle with the Spirit, attempting to let myself be broken open.

As the days of this pilgrimage pass, I'm identifying with Jacob, the grandson of Abraham who wrestled with an angel at a place called Peniel (Gen. 32:24-32). Jacob had had a falling-out with his brother Esau and was now on the cusp of reunion; he was terrified it wouldn't go well. As Jacob spent the night alone, a stranger showed up at his camp, and the two men wrestled all night long. Not knowing who the stranger was, Jacob demanded a blessing from him. The man did so, but not before wrenching Jacob's hip out of its socket. I suppose Jacob walked with a limp for a long time, a reminder of the tussle.

Stephen is saying more about tears — how they cleanse, how

they bring redemption, how they make us whole. It is all so true, so evident in this setting where both glory and unrest rage. As the apostle Paul says, "Work out your own salvation with fear and trembling" (Phil. 2:12).

"We'll go inside now," Stephen tells us. "You'll see the window that frames a view of the Old City. Jesus cried over Jerusalem, and don't we understand why! There is no peace here. Even now. This city needs a prophet for peace!" Stephen's great passion for this place — and for peace — is obvious. "We can only look forward to the New Jerusalem," he says, "where every tear will be wiped away."

Our pilgrim group solemnly enters Dominus Flevit. Because it's configured in the shape of a teardrop, the chapel has a tall, curved exterior and a small, circular interior. The only ornamentation is the panoramic window, which overlooks Jerusalem. The glinting gold of the Dome of the Rock caps the scene.

Was it just one week ago that we toured the Temple Mount and I pondered whether my heart was *sin-cere*? That question has aged; the answer has deepened in the intervening days. I'm seeing that my vocation as a religious leader has formed a kind of cover over my spiritual life. I have given my whole heart to ministry. But have I given my whole heart to God? They are different things.

Framing the panoramic window is a black iron grille that superimposes a communion chalice over Jerusalem, as if the city itself is being lifted up for blessing. How fitting. Jesus was willing to be lifted up in sacrifice as a blessing on all humanity, including the very people and place that would kill him. The image helps me connect ideas that have hung in the background of this pilgrimage: blessing and judgment. I've had such naïve notions of these things, thinking of them as opposites: Blessing is positive, and judgment — in the sense that it's a euphemism for condemnation — is negative. If God blesses us, then we win the lottery, or at least live cancer-free, and end up in heaven. If God judges us, then we flounder to pay our rent, or contract a disease, and end up in eternal torment.

But Jesus' tears over Jerusalem hold blessing and judgment together. He wants to bless, but instead must judge the corruption he sees. Both words, "blessing" and "judgment," describe the dynamic between God and humans. Instead of being opposites, blessing and judgment are inside out from each other. Each is pushing us closer to truth, closer to God. The purpose of divine blessing is to lead the blessed one toward God's presence, toward growth and peace. The purpose of divine judgment is to lead the judged one toward God's presence, toward repentance and renewal.

Jesus is judging Jerusalem with his words, but not because he seeks its destruction; rather, he judges it to provide an opportunity for change. I can only imagine what grief he felt as he looked at Jerusalem. How his heart must have broken over this city. I am an alien here — let's be honest — and yet this city and its lack of peace fill me with sorrow. Jesus spent three years of his life teaching these people, healing them, telling them about the kingdom. For what? He had to wonder.

As a religious leader, I know how crushing it is to cast a vision and wonder if it ever catches. I've poured my heart into my work only, at times, to fail — at least in my own mind. But I don't mean to compare myself to Jesus. My vision for ministry, my hopes, my investment in results — these are all twisted around my personality. My tears easily become self-centered rather than holy.

But Jesus was radically different. Not only the manner of his death but his whole life was a sacrifice. Perhaps these days of pilgrimage, following Jesus from Bethlehem to Nazareth to Jerusalem, have given me new eyes. Did Jesus have to be born at all, laid beside a teenaged mother in a rock manger? Did he have to spend long days repeating his message about the kingdom, only to be misunderstood and ignored? Did he have to spend himself curing broken people? Did he have to be hungry and tired with no place to lay his head? Of course not. So why did he do it? Why did he suffer all the frailties of flesh, of emotion, of broken hopes?

The panorama of the ancient city gives weighted meaning to

Jesus' words. "Jerusalem, Jerusalem, the city that kills the prophets and stones those who are sent to it!" These are reprimand, but aren't they also lament? And a lament is like singing the blues. You don't bother to sing them unless you believe something better is coming. A lament assumes that God is still present.

Timing is the problem, of course. We don't know when lament will become joy. When Jesus was here, he didn't know, either — not if we take his humanity seriously. When will the blues become a happy tune? Scripture gives us pieces of the vision: The world will be peaceful and just, and the lion will lie down with the lamb. All families will live in their own homes, underneath their own vines and fig trees, drawing water from their own wells (Micah 4:3-4; Isaiah 65:20-25). This will be the kingdom of God. This is what we're waiting for. "Thy kingdom come," we pray.

The kingdom will come in God's time, which is not time at all, but eternity. The great eternity will be ushered in by the Blessed One, who comes in the name of the Lord. We will wave palm branches once again for Jesus, the Lord of time. Meanwhile, we are trapped in time, in a world creaking under divine judgment, a world aching for blessing. Yet blessing hovers at the edges because God is present.

As we sit in the Dominus Flevit chapel, someone begins to sing "Jesus, Remember Me." It's a Taize chant that repeats the words of the thief on the cross: "Jesus, remember me when you come into your kingdom" (Luke 23:42). The rest of us take up the melody, repeating the words until it's time for us to get up and leave, to make way for other pilgrims.

🌱   🌱   🌱

We leave the chapel that is shaped like a tear and walk a short way to the Garden of Gethsemane, where Jesus prayed and wept again. The ground is dusty in this garden. Gnarled olive trees are roped off. It's said that the roots of these ancient trees go back two thousand years, to the time of Jesus. Olive trees can live a long time, and these have been well-tended. We go as close as we can to look at the great knobby roots. We pass two enormous round stones, one lying flat and the other upright, propped against it. Both stones are as wide across as a person and as thick as a mattress.

Kyle comments, "The word 'gethsemane' is Hebrew for olive press." I imagine the crushing weight of the stone, the friction of grinding until the olives give up their oil, their golden life-blood.

🌢 🌢 🌢

There is one more church to visit on this hill overlooking Jerusalem: the Church of All Nations (sometimes called the Church of the Rock of the Agony). It's a large, modern church with windows of purple glass. Inside, the colored light tinges the air with sorrow. Up front is the rock where Jesus prayed on the night that he wrestled in prayer. "Father, if you are willing, remove this cup from me; yet, not my will but yours be done" (Luke 22:42). This is the spot where Judas betrayed Jesus with a kiss. I want to go up to the rock and kiss it. I feel a mother's urge to kiss away pain, a lover's urge to show passion, a pilgrim's urge to express devotion.

But I can't get closer to the rock because a Catholic group is celebrating the Eucharist. The priest is ornately robed in red vestments that drip with solemnity. The Catholic tradition knows how to commemorate Jesus as a man of sorrows, which I respect. There are times when we need a crucifix rather than an empty cross, when we feel alone in grief and need to remember that Jesus, too, was a body acquainted with sorrow. I think about my own lifetime of tears, not to dwell on them but to multiply them by every human who has ever lived. What a flood of tears! For the first time I realize how Jesus stood in that flood like a rock, how the river of tears broke around him. *Beautiful*

Jesus was no stranger to pain. He showed us how to pray through pain, trusting in God during the most desperate moments. This is what prayer is for. Prayer is not for asking God for new toys, or fine weather, or a winning game. Prayer is for pouring out our heart and having our hope restored.

The people are singing the "Hosanna" now. I think of the questions I've wrestled with on this pilgrimage, questions I haven't yet wrestled to the ground. Why must we travel through places of pain? Although I can't say I have the answer, the question no longer seems pressing. I'm beginning to understand that pain is part of the human experience, part of the price we pay for being created in the image of God with the ability to choose, in a world where other people make choices, too.

The red-robed priest lifts up the host. This act no longer reminds me of the differences between Catholic and Protestant, but of Jesus' willingness to pay even this price for us: before even the Crucifixion, he paid the price of incarnation, of entering a broken world where every choice will somehow lead to pain.

CHAPTER 19

The Stations of the Cross

*I saw the holy city, the new Jerusalem, coming down out of heaven
from God, prepared as a bride adorned for her husband.*

REVELATION 21:2

I T's PITCH-BLACK WHEN the travel alarm goes off. I groan.
"Here's another reason Presbyterians don't do the Stations
of the Cross," I say to JoAnne in the darkness. "It's too dang
early."

"Wanna skip it?" she asks.

"Don't tempt me!"

"Get thee behind me, Satan?" JoAnne replies. "Or is that what
Charlie would say?"

We both laugh, which helps us get out of bed.

🎋 🎋 🎋

The fact is that no Holy Land pilgrimage would be complete
without walking the Stations of the Cross along the Via Dolorosa, the Way of Sorrows. This is the route Jesus walked from his
condemnation to his crucifixion. For thousands of years, believers
have been retracing these steps and reading Scripture along the
way, at various "stations." Does it matter if it's the exact route
Jesus took or if every station is in the biblical account? This is a
time-honored tradition. If I managed the rest of it — kneeling,

lighting candles, praying at rocks — certainly I can manage to walk a pilgrim path through the streets of Jerusalem.

🎋   🎋   🎋

All forty of us leave Saint George's in the early morning stillness, walking two abreast in silence. We each carry a book with readings, litanies, and hymns. The pilgrim at the front of the procession carries a wooden cross, about four feet tall. Another pilgrim carries a second cross of similar size about halfway down the line. We were given the opportunity to sign up to carry one of the crosses, and we will take turns.

I overhear Jessica ask Brian in a hushed voice, "Should we wait for Shane? I don't see him."

"He's not coming," Brian answers.

"Is he sick?" Jessica's voice is full of concern.

"He's fine. He'd just rather do this by himself, later."

"But he's okay?"

"He just doesn't like all this non-biblical stuff," Brian says. "No problem."

Station I: "Jesus Is Condemned to Death"

As we arrive at the first station in the courtyard at the Monastery of the Flagellation, a cock crows, breaking the silence that has hung over our group for the entire thirty-minute walk. Ten days ago, in this same courtyard full of beautiful blooming flowers, a few of us had met Tercier, the atheist who said it was impossible to believe in God in the Holy Land because religion is just an excuse for hatred. I remember his outrage as I stand in the same spot and listen to the reading from Mark 14, where Jesus is brought before the religious authorities. The high priest asks Jesus, "Are you the Messiah, the son of the Blessed One?" Jesus answers, "I am," and is condemned for blasphemy. We offer prayers of confession for our own tendencies to judge. We also pray for all those involved in the legal process and those imprisoned.

Station II: "Jesus Carries the Cross"

The second stop is another chapel in the same courtyard. JoAnne does the reading from Mark 15, where the people shout, "Crucify him!" As she reads, a calico cat wanders through our group, mewling hungrily. We offer prayers for those who victimize others, or who are victimized, and acknowledge our own tendency to be indifferent to suffering.

Station III: "Jesus Falls for the First Time"

By now the narrow streets are getting noisy. Metal gates squeal as they are unlocked and lifted by shopkeepers. The reading is from Psalm 69:1-2, which is about the deep waters coming up around the neck. This station is extra-biblical because Scripture has no account of Jesus falling. I feel curious about where these traditions come from and what they mean to people. I don't doubt that ancient pilgrims traveling this Via Dolorosa experienced drama and poignancy that we, technology-soaked as we are, fail to appreciate. We offer prayers for those who are weak, or in pain, or experiencing failure.

Station IV: "Jesus Meets His Mother"

This station is also extra-biblical because there is no account of Jesus interacting with Mary at this point. Yet something similar must have happened. The reading is Lamentations 1:12: "See if there is any sorrow like my sorrow." We read a litany using the words of Simeon about a sword piercing Mary's heart. I suddenly realize that my Protestant distance from Mary has protected me from entering the pain she felt as a mother. Even now I am resistant to bridging that distance. I don't want to approach the reality that sometimes a child dies before the parent — the thought is too distressing. An incoherent prayer wraps around my heart: *Lord, my daughters!*

As the group reads a printed prayer together, a young boy, maybe seven years old, walks by, sobbing. He sounds absolutely lost and brushes past us, oblivious in his need. Our prayer is for mothers, fathers, children, and those who are lost. At this point Kyle is carrying the cross, and as we pray, a woman wearing a *hijab* walks up and spits on his shoe. He jumps, and so do I. But then I see our group through her eyes — so many foreigners parading around with enormous crosses — and wonder that we haven't been spit on before now.

Station V: "Simon of Cyrene Helps to Carry Jesus' Cross"

The foot traffic is picking up considerably. The next reading is just one verse, Mark 15:21, about Simon of Cyrene. We read a litany that adds a little flesh to those bare bones. Our prayer is for foreigners and those pressed into service. As we pray, a Coptic priest comes by. His hat, of black felt wool, is a solemn circle atop a face nearly obscured by a bushy gray beard. He wears long black robes which swing as he strides. He's obviously in a hurry, but stops to make the sign of the cross over the cross we're carrying. I feel a stranger's curiosity about him and his gesture, but also a surprising solidarity with this believer in an odd hat.

Station VI: "Veronica Wipes Jesus' Face"

There is no room to stand because all the shops are opening, so we shuffle about as Michael does the reading, which is from Isaiah 53:4: "Surely he has borne our infirmities and carried our diseases." I'm relieved that I wasn't assigned a reading at one of the extra-biblical stations. This station about Veronica feels especially problematic because I can think only about the creation of a cloth, a relic, rather than an actual historic moment. Yet the prayers we offer are for those who have the eyes to see the image of God in others, and this prayer moves me: it is something I struggle to do.

Station VII: "Jesus Falls for the Second Time"

We pass people who are arguing loudly in the street. They are accustomed to seeing groups of pilgrims and pay us no mind. Someone reads Psalm 38:10-11, about strength failing, and I can hardly hear because so many schoolchildren in uniforms and backpacks are streaming by. We offer prayers for mercy, but they are drowned out by the roar of a diesel engine. A tractor-type vehicle is pulling a green cart. Between the tractor and the cart, a man balances on the wobbly hitch while smoking a cigarette — as if this were an easy thing to do. He and I look each other in the eye, and I would laugh if it weren't such a solemn journey, this Via Dolorosa.

Station VIII: "Jesus Rebukes the Daughters of Jerusalem"

The reading is Luke 23:28, where Jesus says, "Do not weep for me, but weep for yourselves and for your children." I can barely focus on the reading and the prayers because a group of pilgrims comes up behind us, then passes through the middle of us. As they pass, someone snaps a flash picture of me because I'm standing beside the plaque marking the station. I blink, and just then two beefy men pass, each one stopping to cross himself before the plaque. The prayers we offer emphasize penitence, and I contemplate what penitence means here and now: what I am sorry for, what the beefy men might be remorseful about, what decisions and indecisions all of us humans regret. Our group moves on, passing a place where a swastika is deeply etched in the stone of the wall. I've heard that the swastika, the broken cross, is an ancient symbol for peace which the Nazis appropriated. If that's true, it seems a perfect symbol for this penitential spot on the Via Dolorosa.

Station IX: "Jesus Falls for the Third Time"

We come out onto the roof of the Church of the Holy Sepulchre. Below us is the bedrock of Golgotha, below that the Stone of Anointing, below that the tomb of Jesus. Above us the sky is bright blue with an almost-full moon still visible. The reading is from Psalm 88, which says that the psalmist's life is at the brink of the grave. The prayers are for those who despair — and those who minister to those who despair. I remember again that the main job of ministers is to be "purveyors of hope," or else we have nothing to offer, nothing at all.

Station X: "Jesus Is Stripped of His Garments"

This station is very close to the previous one. It is 7:30 now, and the bells of the Church of the Holy Sepulchre begin to ring. We can't ignore them because they are very close to us. Each stroke is a triplet, and the ringing lasts a full two minutes. When it's done, the reading resumes, from John 19:24, about the dividing of Jesus' garments. As we pray, the organ from inside the church begins to play. I'm not sure exactly where the organ is, but our feet seem to reverberate with its sound, which accompanies our prayers for those who are stripped of their dignity.

Station XI: "Jesus Is Nailed to the Cross"

We hear a brief reading (Luke 23:40-43) about the thief on the cross. We use a litany that repeats the phrase "Jesus, remember me when you come into your kingdom," which I found so moving just yesterday. But why does the name of this station not mention the thief on the cross? His interactions with Jesus are a vital part of the scriptural story, so why are they given such short shrift? It becomes challenging to concentrate on what's happening because a man comes through a door and begins to fill buckets with water from a hose. The sound of the running water continues throughout our prayers, and he shuts it off just as we finish reading. Then he picks up the two heavy buckets and grunts as he carries them back through the doorway.

Station XII: "Jesus Dies on the Cross"

It's my turn to read, so I hand my water bottle to Kyle to free my hands. I read from John 19, where Jesus says, "I thirst." Out of the corner of my eye I notice Kyle screw the top off my water bottle and take a long drink. I swallow a smile. Kyle is always serious when I'm hungry or tired, and playful when I'm serious. Our prayer is for those who are dying, and for those who minister to the dying. The prayer ends as they all have ended: "Save us and help us, we humbly beseech you, O Lord."

Station XIII: "Jesus Is Given to His Mother"

We go into the Church of the Holy Sepulchre, and pass through a small chapel that is full of icons of Mary. An elderly dark-skinned man in long, black Ethiopian robes leans on a cane and watches us go by. We pass through another chapel and into a different courtyard, then go back inside another section of the church. We are at the bedrock of Golgotha. We pause for a moment, then continue on to the chapel beneath that one, where the bedrock has been split. As we gather tightly in that small space, the organ begins to play — very loudly and triumphantly. The reading is from John 19: Joseph of Arimathea takes the body of Jesus. Our prayer includes, "Holy Mary, Mother of God, pray for us sinners, now, and at the hour of our death." I have heard that prayer used in movies, but have never uttered it myself. Until now.

Station XIV: "Jesus Is Laid in the Tomb"

Marty does the reading from Matthew 27 about putting Jesus' body in the tomb which has been hewn from rock. We pray together: "We see you condemned, we see you stripped, we see you nailed, we see you crucified, we see you buried. Lord Jesus Christ, we come to the empty tomb. And we see our own sin, we see our own tomb, we see our own death, we see our own vacuum." As we read these words, the organ music begins to play again, and I sense that the Spirit of God is filling the church. For the briefest of moments, I glimpse the future reality of my own death, a void into which peace descends. As soon as I think the word "peace," the feeling flees. Perhaps my own mortality is not something I am ready to make peace with, except in the most glancing of ways.

Station XV: "Christ Is Risen. Alleluia!"

For the final station, we move to the top of the passage that leads down to the Armenian chapel. This is where Crusader crosses line the walls, testimony to the hundreds of thousands of pilgrims who have been here before us. It suddenly strikes me that the cross-carvers were probably men. Weren't most of the Crusaders men? Yet I belong here too. I am as full of folly as any Crusader, as full of hope as any pilgrim. Charlie does the reading from John 20, where Mary Magdalene encounters Jesus outside the tomb and thinks he is the gardener. How I love the fact that Jesus appeared to a woman first, and what's more, to a woman blinded by grief. Of course she had trouble opening her tear-filled eyes. Don't we all? Yet her momentary blindness opens the story to me, a woman who has also been blinded by grief at times, a woman who wants desperately to see the risen Jesus.

Our litany and prayer are victorious: "Do not dwell on your wounds, for he has risen to heal you! Alleluia!"

The stations are done.

As the Alleluia fades away, I turn the last page of our booklet, unready to be finished. After the ups and downs of this Via Dolorosa, the finale feels anti-climactic. I had imagined a more majestic setting for the resurrection story, perhaps a prominence overlooking the city, or rugged rock cliffs outlining the brow of a hill. Instead, we are in the bowels of a church. I feel like we've been assembling a jigsaw puzzle and have discovered we're missing the final pieces, right in the center. Perhaps this is why it's called the Via Dolorosa, rather than the Via Resurrection. This way of sorrows is the one we recognize. We can enter the resurrection only by faith — not by sight or experience.

I feel a certain relief as we leave the stone enclosure of the church and emerge into the hot, dusty air. Merchants bustle around their just-opened shops; tourists converse in a cacophony of languages; men stride past in religious garb. I imagine Jesus on the streets of Jerusalem two millennia ago. He is a rabbi, a healer, a prophet. He is a beaten man carrying a cross. He is the resurrected Lord. I blink in the blinding sun. I believe that Jesus is the Savior of the world. In the bustle of this Jerusalem street, perhaps that means more than I'd realized.

CHAPTER 20

Infidel!

I will not let you go unless you bless me.

GENESIS 32:26

A FTER WE FINISH the Stations of the Cross, the whole
group heads across the Old City toward the Jewish Quarter,
where a few sacred sites are clustered together: the Upper Room,
David's Tomb, and the Dormition of Mary.

As we walk, I think about what I'll say at my final interview,
which will be filmed tonight. Brian has asked us to choose a
central Scripture passage to sum up this pilgrimage. It's more
than daunting. I want to say something worthy, even profound.
Something that fits in a sound bite but doesn't sound like a
sound bite.

At least I've settled on which Scripture to use. For the last
day or so I've been thinking about Jacob wrestling with the
angel. It's rather an odd text, mainly because it's not clear why
the angel has come to Jacob, or why the two of them are fighting, but the crux of the text seems to be Jacob saying, "I will
not let you go unless you bless me." For me, this pilgrimage has
been an extended time of divine wrestling. I want to receive a
blessing, but it isn't so easy. I'm forced to face sides of myself I
would rather ignore: my prejudices, my blind spots, my tendency
toward self-righteousness. I almost feel like the pilgrimage itself

is an angel wrestling me into another way of being, but I haven't reaped the blessing yet.

The funny thing is that last night when I asked JoAnne which passage she'd chosen, she mentioned this same one. It seemed an odd coincidence. The Bible is a thick book, and we chose the same few verses — which haven't been mentioned during the ten days of pilgrimage. I'd like to ask her more about why she chose this Scripture. What has she wrestled with?

As we walk across the Old City to visit our last few sites, Charlie is taking his turn carrying the four-foot cross. I glance at him, curious how this day has been for him. His face is serene.

I ask, "This was your first time doing the Stations of the Cross, right? So what did you think of it?"

"Powerful. The Evil One is everywhere." He clasps the cross to his chest. "What about you? Wasn't it your first time too?"

"It was. I'm still wrestling with some things."

"Satan will do that to you," Charlie says.

"Satan, or an angel," I answer. "But how about you? What are you wrestling with?"

"You mean today or any day?"

"I mean this whole pilgrimage. What have you wrestled with?"

Charlie ponders the question. "Nothing." He shakes his head. "Really, I can't say I've wrestled with anything. This trip has just confirmed what I already believed."

I guess there are many kinds of pilgrims.

🐜   🐜   🐜

We arrive in the Jewish Quarter. The Upper Room is the place where Jesus celebrated Passover with his disciples shortly before one of the disciples, Judas, betrayed him to the religious authorities, an action that led directly to Jesus' death. Before we enter the room, Stephen gives details, but I only half-listen. I just want to picture Jesus here with his disciples.

The room is large, with high arches creating a two-story-high ceiling. The room is full of pilgrims, but empty of furniture, altars, hanging lamps, and the other accoutrements of shrines. How refreshing. As I try to imagine Jesus at a table with his disciples, the members of another large pilgrim group — Americans — begin to sing praise music, complete with guitar accompaniment. It feels like they're using up all the air in the spacious room. I can hardly breathe, much less feel the breath of the Spirit.

We wait politely for the song to finish, then walk a short way to David's Tomb. David was a pivotal figure in Hebrew Scripture, the great shepherd-king of Israel and Judah. But, because the authenticity of the tomb is contested, this tomb is a minor site. It's owned, or at least controlled, by a yeshiva, a school to teach Jewish boys Torah and Talmud. Perhaps the rules are laid down by the yeshiva; whatever the case, women aren't allowed into the main area of the tomb. Men may enter — and it doesn't matter whether they're Jewish or not, mind you, just that they're male. There's a little way station we women may visit, a place to peek at what the men are doing. This is explained as a matter of course. It reminds me of the Western Wall, where women stand on chairs to peer over the divider and see their boys bar-mitzvahed.

The rules aren't unexpected, and I don't even care about David's tomb! But I do care that I'm not allowed to enter it because of my gender. The prohibitions call to mind all the misogynist messages that have been declaimed to me by religious men in authority, words that surge into my memory — and into my body. I spout off to the video camera, even though I'm tired and not particularly eloquent. The blank lens reflects my anger back to me even as it records my words. I hesitate, not because I've expressed my complaint, but because this snippet might find its way into the documentary. I'll look like an overly emotional woman, which just feeds the misogyny. To stop myself, I leave.

Outside the entrance to David's tomb, Kyle is leaning on the four-foot cross. "Patriarchy is alive and well here," I tell him.

"And that surprises you?" he answers, laughing.

"Ha-ha. That's easy for you to say. You're a tall white-haired man. I bet you're the kind of priest who wears a collar to mow the lawn."

Kyle laughs again, and we start walking toward the next site with the group. Kyle is carrying the cross. "Believe me," he says, "you really didn't miss much at that tomb. You've seen one tomb, you've seen 'em all, right? And I thought you were about full up with candles and shrines, anyway."

"I am," I say. "I'm almost full up with meaningful moments. Maybe I'm just ready to go home and see my family."

Our group has reached the day's final stop, the Dormition of Mary. "This is an Orthodox site," Stephen explains. "'Dormition' means 'sleep' and refers to the tradition that the Virgin Mary didn't die, but fell asleep and was taken up into heaven." He swoops his arms upward with his palms facing up.

"I know I'm tired," I say to Kyle, "but I've never even heard of this doctrine about Mary."

He laughs. "Spoken like a Protestant. I guess there's some that venerates the Virgin, and some that doesn't. Me — I can go either way."

"Spoken like an Anglican," I say. "Both sides against the middle. Or are you hedging your bets? Maybe you just don't like to admit when a doctrine is preposterous."

"A doctrine — 'preposterous'?" he asks. "You mean like the Resurrection?"

I look at his pseudo-serious face and burst out laughing. "I get your point. Three days dead in a tomb."

"It's what belief *is*," he tells me. "Preposterous."

Inside the Dormition shrine, two circular staircases lead to a crypt. We descend to an underground room that's as quiet as, well, a tomb. In the center is a life-sized effigy of Mary in repose, her hands crossed on her chest. She is lying atop a coffin of some kind, as if in perpetual sleep.

It's been a long day of great gravity. So many thoughts are stirred up, incomplete. I've had to clamp down my impulses many times. Feeling a bit feisty now, I whisper to Kyle, "She looks like Sleeping Beauty."

"Definitely," he whispers back, a smile dancing across his face. "Part Vatican. Part Disney."

The urge to laugh in a holy place is absolutely devilish. I try to swallow my snickering, but the sound ricochets around the marble walls. A guard thumps down the stairs, scowling. I cover my mouth and bolt back up the staircase Kyle and I have just descended. As I burst into the open air, a guard reprimands me in a stern voice. "Down, not Up!"

From the other side of the shrine, Kyle joins me, having come placidly up the proper staircase. "Going the wrong way, pilgrim?" he asks.

🐛 🐛 🐛

Our large group begins the long walk back toward Saint George's campus. The distance is more than a mile, so we begin to straggle out, though there are still two people carrying the large crosses at the front and back ends of our file. JoAnne and I walk in silence companionably. Suddenly there's a gush and spray as something explodes at our feet. Before I can register what it is, there's a second hit. My pants are now drenched from the knees down. JoAnne and I glance at each other in disbelief, then look up. There's a second-story window open to the air, but barred. On the other side is a group of about five girls, giggling. They're wearing school uniforms and look like eighth-graders. Another water balloon comes sailing down and hits the wall opposite us.

"Hey, girls!" JoAnne calls up. "What are you doing?"

One of the girls yells, "It's disgusting!"

"What is?"

"The cross," yells the vocal girl. "I want to vomit it up!"

I step backward, literally taken aback. The preacher in me wants to chastise them. The teacher in me wants to engage them. The mother in me wants to ignore their bad behavior. But the believer in me simply feels hurt, as if I have been struck square in the chest with those ridiculous water balloons.

JoAnne resumes walking. "It's what they've been taught," she says. "That's all it is."

I catch up to her and agree. "They probably do it every day. Lunch-time entertainment."

"Right. Buy Doritos from the vending machine. Then throw water bombs at the Christian pilgrims." She laughs.

I try to laugh but still feel rattled. "Well, if this had to happen, I'm glad it happened on the Via Dolorosa."

"Right," says JoAnne. "Humiliation for the sake of a cross."

🐝   🐝   🐝

After lunch, we have the afternoon off. Tomorrow is our last day; we fly out of Tel Aviv late tomorrow night. This is our last opportunity to spend time in Jerusalem. Nobody else is interested in walking back in to the city, so I decide to go alone. Perhaps I'm a spiritual glutton, but I don't want to waste these last few hours.

Since I'm done seeing pilgrim sights, I unwrap the scarf I've been wearing around my waist as a handy head covering. Even these few extra layers of silk made me sweat. While I'm at it, I decide to take off my long pants and put on the shorts I brought for the Dead Sea day. I feel better as I cool down. If I'm off the pilgrim clock, maybe I can go back to being an American woman and admit I own a pair of legs. My shorts feel blessedly cool. A little sneaky, but cool. I grab my journal and head to the Damascus Gate.

The Muslim Quarter feels much friendlier than it used to, now that it's familiar. I tromp over streets of paving stone, noticing details about the people bustling around me. I stop to examine the colorful wares of street-sellers. The tables displaying women's underwear no longer shock me. The fragrant heaps of spices are enticing, and I purchase some saffron as a gift for my husband. The aroma from the falafel stand is tantalizing. That means my stomach is feeling better! I decide to be daring and buy some fresh dates. I love to eat them dried, so why not try these? The plump orange orbs are the most perfect fruit I have ever put in my mouth. When I bite down, the meat of the date feels substantial but then gives way to the perfect combination of softness and chewiness — all exploding with sugar.

My senses are so consumed with taking in Jerusalem that my mind becomes unleashed. My thoughts flow and come together in new ways. I feel strangely at home. I remember how, as I embarked on this pilgrimage, I worried about the violence I might encounter — not the threat of bodily harm, but the threat of what new ideas might do to my belief system. A few water balloons turned out to be the worst of the physical violence! Perhaps the most difficult part is facing the fact that those girls and I have much in common. What's so different about what they're being taught and what I was taught? In my Reformed upbringing, we were taught to be polite, but that's only a surface issue. We too were children of the covenant, set apart. We felt superior. It's ugly to say it straight out like that, but it's true. We didn't mix with "the world." And isn't it this sense of rightness — righteousness, purity — that feeds violence? Don't we believe that God loves the righteous more?

Perhaps the act of tracing my finger over the nameless Crusader crosses helped me work out this religious impulse toward high-mindedness, this passion for righteousness. But why lay that passion at the feet of the Crusaders a thousand years ago? This passion isn't dead. Look at my own Calvinism. Our Pilgrim and Puritan forebears believed that they were a chosen people decreed to establish a shining city on a hill, and that belief shut out other beliefs, not from malice but from the desire for purity. If you've got something shining and pure that belongs to God, you need to safeguard it.

No wonder I was worried about coming to this Holy Land. It was an absolutely reasonable fear. Religious zeal leads to a passion for purity which leads to violence in some organic way. And that fact should terrify people of faith.

But how can I think I'm above this messy combination? Even on this pilgrimage I've been irritated with my fellow pilgrims for not believing exactly as I do, even though we share the same faith. Don't I sometimes act as if I'm right? Even irreproachable? The truth is, there is in my core a certain intransigence, a belief that my flavor of Christianity is the best flavor.

I take a seat at an outdoor café table and order a Turkish coffee.

A boy brings the handleless cup and saucer on a round silver tray. As I sip, I write down the word "passion," a word that can mean such different things: religious zeal, sexual desire, enthusiasm, love, violence. Jesus' suffering and death. This morning's walk along the Via Dolorosa is still echoing in my soul. I trace a cross beside the word "passion." Certainly all of these meanings come from the same root. In this Holy Land they have a motley co-existence. Why should we be surprised when one passion ignites another? For good and for bad, we can't get away from these connections. The passions are all stitched together, and the seams simply show here in a more pronounced way than they do back home. And I can't pretend that somehow my religious motivations are above the fray, or purer than anyone else's.

In the face of all this, to believe in the possibility of redemption is truly a statement of faith.

The coffee is bitter, overpowering even the sweetness of the dates that lingers on my tongue.

Why did I come on this pilgrimage? I need to be able to tell the camera tonight. I write it down: *I came on this pilgrimage because I wanted to move deeper into my calling. But I'm seeing that my vocational call — ministry — has in some ways eclipsed the more personal call to discipleship.*

On the one hand, I've been following Jesus my whole life. I couldn't NOT follow Jesus. Sometimes it's even been irritating because a nagging question has surfaced: Where is my free will? Could I even have chosen a different path? But now I'm seeing deeper layers. Perhaps the call is to live as a disciple, as a forgiven person, and to offer the same to others.

When I began this pilgrimage, I didn't know I needed to find forgiveness! I thought I already had it. This pilgrimage has turned up surprises. It's like finding out that your house has a rotting basement when you've been happily living in the upstairs, sitting by a sunny window. I'll leave the declaration that I am the chief of sinners to the apostle Paul. But the difficult truth is that I do sin — daily: I don't view the world with the eyes of Christ; I don't look everywhere for the face of Christ; I don't show the world the face of Christ; I don't live what I pray: Thy Kingdom come.

I can't articulate everything I've learned. But I do know that when I return home, I must not cease to be a pilgrim. I need to figure out how to take up the roles I've temporarily set aside — wife and mother and minister — without dropping this new role as pilgrim.

My coffee cup is empty. My pilgrim cup overflows with whirling thoughts, both bitter and sweet. It's time to head back to Saint George's. Maybe along the way I'll find clarity. Maybe back in my room I'll write some profound sentences to use in the interview. Maybe I'll even have time for a nap.

I pay the bill and head toward Saint George's. I'm footsore by the time I spy the familiar gate. Beneath the tree limbs are the chairs where Khalil and I sat and talked just ten days ago. Waiting for the light to change, I notice two young boys — seven or eight years old — who are horsing around on the street corner. One of them has a wooden bat, which he swings, low. Suddenly he notices me and abruptly stops moving. He stares at my legs. I become uncomfortably aware that my knees show. He points, yelling in a high pitch to the other. They begin shouting at me, angrily. The one with the bat comes at me, raising the weapon over his head with both hands. He is moving in slow motion. My feet freeze. I'm mesmerized by watching what he intends to do. Would he really harm me? Deliberately, he holds the bat high, then brings it down. I pull away in time, and the bat makes a wide swoop over my right shoulder. I can hardly believe what's happened.

Meanwhile, the other boy has found a large stick. My heart is racing. When the boy with the bat raises his weapon again, I find my feet and sprint across the street without looking for traffic. Vehicles honk and swerve. In a moment I'm within the protection of Saint George's gates. I don't stop running until I'm in the refuge of my dorm room and can collapse on the bed.

Why had it not occurred to me that I am an outrage? There are two sides to every notion of religious purity, and my exposed knees are the proof that I am on the wrong side. I am the infidel.

Oh angel, is that my hip that's been knocked out of joint?

CHAPTER 21

Open

Then their eyes were opened, and they recognized him.

LUKE 24:31

W E ENDED YESTERDAY's Stations of the Cross with the
Resurrection story, so today we're headed to Emmaus,
to see the site of one of the best-loved post-Resurrection stories.
(Find the whole story in Luke 24:13-35.)

The Emmaus story takes place that first Easter evening while
the word is still spreading that Jesus' tomb is empty. No one
knows what this means. Two of Jesus' followers — Cleopas and a
friend — are walking from Jerusalem to their home in Emmaus.
They are in turmoil, their high hopes for this Jesus destroyed. As
they walk along, Jesus joins them, but hides himself from their
recognition. The two men take him for a stranger who somehow
doesn't know what's been going on in Jerusalem. They tell him
about the recent events, and why they feel so despondent.

The incognito Jesus says to the two men, "How foolish you
are and slow of wit!" Then, still without revealing himself, he in-
terprets the Hebrew Scripture, explaining why this Jesus needed
to suffer before he could enter into glory. When they reach their
destination, the two friends press the stranger to stay the night
with them, and he agrees. During supper, the hidden Jesus picks
up the bread and breaks it, and in a miraculous moment, the two

friends realize who he is. Scripture says it simply: "Then their eyes were opened, and they recognized him." Immediately, he vanishes. Cleopas and his friend say to each other, Why didn't we know? Weren't our hearts burning within us while he interpreted the scriptures? *John Wesley*

It's a beautiful story, one of my favorites. The whole time that the men felt so dispirited, the risen Christ had been walking alongside them. Astounding. I'm eager to get to the site to soak in the story. I want to have my own eyes opened, want to feel my own heart burn.

But first there's a final lecture, entitled "Where Is the Site of Emmaus?"

"There are many possible answers to that question," Stephen says. "Holy places move."

The text gives the distance from Jerusalem to Emmaus in stadia, which is an ancient unit of measurement. Different manuscripts list different distances: some say 60 stadia; others say 160. On top of that, it's not known which direction Cleopas and his friend were walking in. Finally, it's not known whether the figure was calculated for one-way or round-trip. In the end, there are four possible locations for Emmaus. As Stephen lists and explains these four possibilities, I avoid looking at Shane. I don't want to see his pained expression during all these calculations. Eventually Stephen says, "After all the evidence is weighed, the most widely recognized site is not the one that's most visited, for a variety of reasons, mainly convenience. The most visited site is called Abu Ghosh. And that's where we're headed today."

To sum up: We have spent an hour hearing which site is most authentic and have decided not to go there! It seems an appropriate end to a Holy Land pilgrimage. Authenticity is in the eye, and heart, of the pilgrim, not in geography.

❦ ❦ ❦

Abu Ghosh is a stone church built in the Crusader period. It's a large structure, but nothing fancy — just great chunks of stone reaching high to a few small windows. We pilgrims enter and wander around, admiring the way the shafts of light penetrate the dungeon-like interior. The walls contain vestiges of colorful frescoes. There's an enormous altar, which our leaders set up for communion. We sit down on wooden pews, and the worship service begins.

Stephen asks us to reflect on this question: Where have we encountered Jesus during the ten days of this pilgrimage? If we'd like to, we may share our thoughts with the others. Pilgrims mention various moments: lighting a candle at the Church of the Nativity in Bethlehem; being deep underground at the tombs in the Church of the Holy Sepulchre; floating in the Dead Sea after the cable-car fiasco at Masada; touring the Deheshieh refugee camp.

Krisha speaks up, very distressed. She had come on this pilgrimage expressly because she wanted to walk along the shore of the Sea of Galilee and see Jesus there. Well, we had been in the Galilee for three nights, and she didn't see Jesus! She cries as she speaks. My heart goes out to her, but I'm surprised. I remember the night of swimming in the Sea of Galilee. Wasn't Jesus there in our laughter? Our unity?

One of the things I cherish about the Reformed tradition is the conviction that we do not control the Spirit of God. The Spirit will appear when the Spirit chooses to appear; all we can do is keep our eyes open. To me, this is what the Emmaus story is all about. I love this peek-a-boo quality of Jesus, as if he's saying, "Now you see me — now you don't!"

JoAnne says, "To me this pilgrimage has been like opening a children's pop-up book. It's taken all the biblical stories I love, and thought I knew, and made them three-dimensional. I see so much more."

She's right. There's something so hands-on about pilgrimage, so unavoidably tactile. It reminds me of dress-shopping with my daughters. You can look at pictures of dresses all you want, but what you must do is actually try them on. You must see whether the shape flatters you, how the fabric drapes on your body, if the colors work against your skin tone. But if you go shopping and know exactly what the dress should look like — the color, the cut, the fabric — you're likely to come home empty-handed. Your mind must be open. Sometimes people say you need to let the dress find you.

Pilgrimage takes a similar kind of openness. Experiencing Jesus is not something we order up but something we allow to happen. We create the space, the heart-space, and the Spirit chooses when and how to appear. We recognize it when it happens.

Stephen begins to preach. First he speaks about the absence and presence of Jesus in the post-Resurrection stories generally: he calls it a "theology of the enigmatic Christ." I suppose that sounds better than "peek-a-boo Jesus." The recurring theme is that Jesus appears and disappears. The people who see Jesus tell others, and those who didn't see must decide whether or not to believe those who did. Jesus seems most apt to appear when the faithful are together in conversation, or in prayer, or in breaking bread. We can do these things, but we cannot command his appearance. Meanwhile, Jesus is forever moving forward, inviting us to follow.

After all — and as Stephen says this, I see how fundamental this is, but slippery to grasp — isn't the very absence of Jesus, in a sense, beckoning us forward? When Jesus appears and disappears, doesn't he encourage us to keep moving toward him? It's like stepping toward a light switch in a dark but familiar room. You know the light is there, so you keep moving forward even though you can't quite see. In a sense, there is no such thing as Jesus' disappearance; there is only our continual movement into a new kind of divine presence. Sanctification

I think about my pocket-sized Jesus, the one I felt I'd outgrown when this pilgrimage began. I'm glad to let that go, but it's not easy to follow this larger, enigmatic Jesus. I see how tempting it is to nail him down, so to speak, to trap him in our theology.

Stephen reminds us what Cleopas and his friend said to each other: "Were not our hearts burning within us while he was talking to us on the road?" He tells us that a pilgrim pays attention to what makes the heart burn. A pilgrim tends the flame. How will we do that when this pilgrimage is ended? He closes by saying that we'll spend ten minutes in silent meditation. He sits down, and a great silence engulfs the group.

This pilgrimage has been like exercising a muscle that sometimes cramps up. It would be easier to stop. I'm not used to approaching God in this way. I want to think my old way, that there is something I can do, something good, and then God will be pleased and give me a reward.

Have I been thinking cause-and-effect without even knowing it? I learned to approach God with my mind, and perhaps this is the result. I like to be logical. Maybe my ancestors were like this, too. Maybe this is why we are Reformed. We are happiest with a complete theological system: beginning, middle, and end, yes with all the main actors playing their appropriate roles. If, at the last minute, the system doesn't quite work, we can quickly say, "Oh well, that's a divine mystery."

How foolish we are, and slow of wit!

What would happen if I forgot everything I thought I knew and began in mystery? I pull out my notebook to write down the few things I know about God, the sureties I'd stake my life on. They are all mysteries:

God created the world. God made us humans, limited, but with the ability to choose. God allows evil in the world, even great evil. But there is also love. Out of love, God entered the world in Jesus. The world couldn't stand that, tried to stamp it out. But love continues. It is the lifeblood of the church. Love will eclipse time.

I close my pilgrim notebook. These simple sentences are all I know, but they are enough. I don't have to chase after Jesus demanding more.

The chaplain stands up, breaking the deep silence. He makes the invitation to the table: "People shall come from north and south, from east and west, to sit at table in the Kingdom of God." He offers the Great Prayer of Thanksgiving, then picks up the round loaf of bread. He says, "When our Lord was at table, he took bread, blessed and broke it." My eyes follow as his hands deliberately tear the loaf and hold the two halves aloft. "Then their eyes were opened, and they recognized him."

He picks up the pitcher and chalice and pours, the wine a red stream into the cup. He picks up the full chalice in one hand, the torn bread in the other, and holds them out to us. "These are the gifts of God for the people of God."

People begin to go forward. I am in a front pew, so I get in line. I tear off a large chunk of bread and dunk one corner into the cup. The sopping part of the bread is aromatic, and the rest is dense. I chew slowly, relishing this taste of heaven. *Yes!*

Then I return to my seat and watch the other pilgrims go forward, their faces expectant and full of hope. I'm surprised when, beside me, Kyle breaks the silence by singing. His tenor voice quavers in the air. After each line he pauses, and the rest of us sing the line back.

> *Are not our hearts burning within us?*
> *Are not our hearts lighted with fire?*
> *Jesus is the Lord!*

The sound of our voices resonates through the stone chamber. I look up at the sunlight streaming through the high windows. I can almost see our song hanging like the dust motes that speckle the rays of light.

It is time to rise for the Benediction, but I don't want to stand up. When I rise from the rough pew, the pilgrimage will be over; I'm already feeling its absence. Of course, we pilgrims have our good-byes to make. We will take final photos. We will celebrate at our farewell dinner. We will part as friends. But with the end of this communion service, we will be done worshiping together.

It will be up to us whether or not we remain pilgrims.

Shalom, Salaam, Peace.

Questions on Pilgrim Themes

Theme 1: Be Open

A pilgrim is open to where the Spirit leads, even if it's uncomfortable.

• In Chapters 1 and 2, Ruth wrestles with the transition from her normal life to this pilgrimage. She must leave certain things behind in order to open herself and become a pilgrim. When have you had to leave something behind? What is something that you need to practice leaving behind?

• In Chapter 15, the pilgrims visit Tabgha, where Jesus multiplied the loaves and fishes. Ruth feels the Spirit invite her to a new way of approaching her words/writing, which involves both release and multiplication. What in your life needs to be released? What needs to be multiplied? Which process is up to us?

• In Chapter 16, Ruth is moved when she listens to a sermon about the healing of a man who is deaf and mute. Have you ever struggled to open your ears to a message that was painful to hear? What was that process like for you, and where did it lead?

• In Chapter 18, the pilgrims visit Dominus Flevit, a chapel shaped like a teardrop. Do you believe that tears can open the heart? Have you cried tears of anguish that felt sacred?

Tears of joy, relief, release? How has the experience of crying affected your spiritual life?

• In Chapter 21, the pilgrims take communion at Emmaus, where Jesus "had been made known to them in the breaking of the bread" (Luke 24:35). Have you experienced an opening of your heart/eyes/ears/tongue through a sacrament or holy ritual of some kind? When has place or setting affected your ability to be open to the Spirit?

Theme 2: Cheek to Cheek

A pilgrim has the opportunity to brush against the presence of the Divine.

• In Chapter 3, the pilgrims hear a lecture about Jerusalem, but, for Ruth, the facts drop away, and the Holy One becomes present when she ducks under an olive tree. How have you experienced the divine presence through the natural world?

• In Chapter 10, Ruth stands in a sheepfold in Bethlehem and hears a familiar text as if for the first time. How did you react to this scene? Have you ever encountered a familiar text or a spiritual truth that suddenly seemed completely new and powerful?

• In Chapter 13, the pilgrims visit Masada. Have you had desert experiences that have made you aware of the presence or absence of God? How did the story of the cable-car mishap make you feel? Have you experienced your own fragility and contingency in a similar way? Does that have any relationship to your spiritual life?

• In Chapter 14, the pilgrims swim in the Sea of Galilee, which Ruth describes as brushing against the Divine. What was your reaction to this experience? Has the touch of water ever been playfully sacred to you?

• In Chapter 17, the pilgrims ascend Mount Tabor, the scene of the Transfiguration. How do you react to the biblical stories that describe Elijah, Moses, or Jesus as radiant like the sun? How appealing or unappealing is it to encounter a prophet, a religious leader, or a divine being? Do you think that supernatural or prophetic encounters occur in our world today? If so, can you think of any examples?

Theme 3: Religious Strangers

A pilgrim cannot avoid the painful connection between religious strangers and estrangement, which sometimes leads to violence, both historically and currently.

• In Chapter 4, Ruth converses with Khalil and discovers the "six degrees of separation" between them. How are you aware of degrees of separation between you and members of different faith traditions? How can a sense of strangeness lead to estrangement, or be overcome? Have you ever become aware of closer connections with people of other faith traditions than you had initially realized?

• In Chapter 5, the pilgrims visit Jerusalem. The atheist Tercier says, "Religion is good for nothing but hatred." Do you agree or disagree? Does religious belief offer any hope? How might we live in such a way as to contradict Tercier's statement? A Muslim shopkeeper says, "We all worship the same God. We are all brothers and sisters." Do you agree or disagree? How do you experience your sisterhood/brotherhood with people of other faiths?

• In Chapters 7-9, the pilgrims visit the Jerusalem shrines of three religious traditions. Have you ever visited a holy site for a faith you do not embrace? What was that like? Are these visits a good idea? How do you react to the Crusader history, which has left its marks in the Holy Land?

• In Chapter 11, Ruth haggles with a street-seller in Bethlehem. Have you ever tried to connect with someone who is very different from you by buying something from them? Did the encounter increase or decrease a sense of estrangement?

• In Chapter 12, the pilgrims visit a Palestinian refugee camp. How do you react to the facts given by the guide, Jihad? How important is it for people of faith to be knowledgeable about what's happening politically in the Holy Land?

• In Chapter 20, Ruth encounters two Muslim boys who run at her with sticks. Have you ever interacted with people who thought you were an infidel? Have you ever interacted with persons whom you regarded as infidels? Can you describe these interactions? What do you think is the link between religious belief and violence? What does the last line of the chapter imply?

Questions for Bible Study

Chapter 1: Uproot Me

I am the bread of life. (John 6:48)

This is the first of seven "I Am" statements of Jesus (chapters 8–15 in the book of John). What does it mean to you that Jesus is the bread of life? In what way do you experience Jesus as bread? How does communion feed you? How has communion functioned to welcome people in, or keep people out?

Chapter 2: Time like Sand

By faith Abraham obeyed when he was called to set out for a place that he was to receive as an inheritance; and he set out, not knowing where he was going. (Hebrews 11:8)

This verse in Hebrews refers to the story of God calling Abram/Abraham to go somewhere unknown (Genesis 12). The story of Abraham's call is foundational to the three great monotheistic traditions. How does that commonality strike you? In what way do you relate to this story? How is this a pilgrim text?

Chapter 3: Olive Trees and Sparrows

Look at the birds of the air; they neither sow nor reap nor gather into barns, and yet your heavenly Father feeds them. (Matthew 6:26)

Ruth slips under an olive tree and remembers this Scripture from the Sermon on the Mount (chapters 5–7 in Matthew). What do you learn from "the birds of the air"? In your life right now, what are you "gathering into barns"? When you consider the whole Sermon on the Mount, do Jesus' words seem to be more about right doctrine or right practice? How do either of these relate to pilgrimage?

Chapter 4: Six Degrees

They confessed that they were strangers and foreigners on the earth, for people who speak in this way make it clear that they are seeking a homeland. (Hebrews 11:13-14)

Hebrews 11 and 12 are chapters about faith. As people of faith, we are all pilgrims. This verse seems to ask, Does faith provide a homeland, or is faith the path of seeking a homeland? How does your faith guide your actions when you encounter other "strangers and foreigners on the earth"?

Chapter 5: Opposing Forces

From one ancestor [God] made all nations to inhabit the whole earth . . . so that they would search for God and perhaps grope for him and find him — though indeed he is not far from each one of us. (Acts 17:26-27)

In Acts 17, the apostle Paul is preaching to the Greeks, seeking points of commonality with his hearers. In what way does this

verse help you connect with Paul or his hearers? How does
this verse speak to you as a pilgrim? How far, or near, is God?
Do you consider yourself to be a seeker, or a finder, of God?

CHAPTER 6: COMPELLED

As a captive to the Spirit, I am on my way to Jerusalem, not know-
ing what will happen to me there. (Acts 20:22)

In Acts 20 the apostle Paul acknowledges the difficult road
that lies ahead of him, which is nevertheless unavoidable.
When have you felt driven by God to do something that you
knew might lead to difficulties? For you as a pilgrim, how does
this verse give you sustenance for the difficult pilgrim path?

CHAPTER 7: SIN-CERE

Lord, my heart is not proud. (Psalm 131:1)

Psalm 131 is one of the Pilgrim Psalms (Psalms 120–134). It
is one of the briefest and most humble of the Psalms. How
does this language of humility resonate with your spiritual life,
especially your prayer life? What new meaning might it have
for you as a pilgrim? A Christian lives in humility while still
proclaiming faith in Christ. How do you experience this ten-
sion, or resolve it?

Chapter 8: Sisters

Jesus, Son of David, have mercy on me! (Mark 10:47)

In Mark 10 Jesus heals a blind beggar named Bartimaeus, who calls out for mercy. When has your heart echoed this beggar's cry? How might the repetition of this cry further open a pilgrim's heart? What thoughts or feelings surface when you pray the "Jesus Prayer"?

Chapter 9: Stone Cold

Come to him, a living stone . . . and let yourselves be built into a spiritual house, to be a holy priesthood. (1 Peter 2:4-5)

The book of First Peter can be read as a series of instructions to new disciples. In what way does the image of "living stone" speak to you as a disciple? What does it mean to you that God might build you into a structure greater than yourself? Stones are common in the Bible, and omnipresent in the Holy Land. What do stones represent?

Chapter 10: Birth and Death

I am the gate for the sheep. (John 10:7)

This verse is another of the "I Am" statements of Jesus. It also calls to mind Psalm 23, which is the "Shepherd Psalm." How have you experienced the shepherding quality of Jesus? How are you like a sheep or a goat? Remember the swaddling cloths. How does a shepherd tend the transition between life and death?

Chapter 11: Love Is Difficult

For now we see in a mirror, dimly, but then we will see face to face. Now I know only in part; then I will know fully, even as I have been fully known. And now faith, hope, and love abide, these three; and the greatest of these is love. (1 Corinthians 13:12-13)

First Corinthians 13 is the great chapter on love. What new meanings come to mind as you consider this chapter in the context of the Israeli/Palestinian conflict? How might a pilgrim be both nourished and challenged by this verse?

Chapter 12: The Hope

How very good and pleasant it is when kindred live together in unity! (Psalm 133:1)

Psalm 133 is one of the Pilgrim Psalms (Psalms 120–134). It is a brief Psalm about unity. What is your experience of unity, or disunity, within communities of faith? How important is unity for you as a pilgrim? How might a pilgrim seek unity? Is it possible for a community of faith to live in unity without demanding conformity (or uniformity) on doctrinal matters?

Chapter 13: Suspension

In my distress I cry to the LORD, that he may answer me. (Psalm 120:1)

Psalm 120 is one of the Pilgrim Psalms (Psalms 120–134). It is a Psalm of lamentation. How comfortable or uncomfortable are you with lamentation? What events have pushed you to lament to God? How are the Psalms helpful when a person is faced with death?

Chapter 14: Flotilla

Where do you get that living water? (John 4:11)

John 4 tells the story of Jesus' encounter with the woman at the well. What surprises you about their entire conversation? In what way do you relate to that woman? In the life of faith, both individually and communally, what is water good for? How does Jesus become living water to you as a pilgrim?

Chapter 15: Multiply

How many loaves have you? Go and see. (Mark 6:38)

The miracle of the multiplication of the loaves and fishes is recounted in Mark 6 (and also in Matthew 14, Luke 9, and John 6). Imagine yourself in the role of different characters in this story: the boy with the lunch, the disciples, the hungry crowd. Which character resonates with you today? How might the world look different if we followed Jesus' example and intentionally moved away from a framework of scarcity and fear and embraced a framework of abundance and generosity? How might this change of attitude affect the conflict in the Holy Land over resources like space and water?

Chapter 16: Cheek to Cheek

Ephphatha! Be opened! (Mark 7:34)

In Mark 7, Jesus heals a man who is deaf and mute. When have you experienced a "release" like this man did when his tongue was loosened? Have you ever experienced being closed down, or sealed? "I was blind but now I see." If you were to be healed, what would change?

Chapter 17: Transform

We ourselves heard this voice come from heaven while we were with him on the holy mountain. (2 Peter 1:18)

In the first chapter of Second Peter, the apostle Peter reflects on his experience at the Transfiguration, which is recounted in the Gospels (Matthew 17, Mark 9, Luke 9). In what ways do you connect — or fail to connect — with Peter's experience of glory, and the way it shaped his life? As a pilgrim, how receptive are you to glory? Why?

Chapter 18: Weep

Jerusalem, Jerusalem, the city that kills the prophets and stones those who are sent to it! (Matthew 23:37)

In Matthew 23, Jesus laments over Jerusalem before he enters it at the beginning of Holy Week. In what way is Jesus' lamentation specific to his time and place? In what way does Jesus show us how to bring laments of all types before God? What beliefs or actions cause Jesus to weep today?

Chapter 19: The Stations of the Cross

I saw the holy city, the new Jerusalem, coming down out of heaven from God, prepared as a bride adorned for her husband. (Revelation 21:2)

Revelation 21 gives us John's vision of the New Jerusalem, which is one of the Bible's final scenes. How has this vision affected your journey of faith? If you have experienced the Stations of the Cross, how has that affected your spiritual life? Does this verse seem like a disconnect with this chapter? If you were asked to select a theme verse for this chapter, what would you choose?

Chapter 20: Infidel!

I will not let you go unless you bless me. (Genesis 32:26)

In Genesis 32, Jacob wrestles with an angel. When have you wrestled with God or one of the angels? In what ways has your hip been put out of joint by such an encounter? A wound such as this can last for a lifetime. Is this a blessing or a curse or both?

Chapter 21: Open

Then their eyes were opened, and they recognized him. (Luke 24:31)

Luke 24 tells about Jesus' appearances after his resurrection. In the Emmaus story, two disciples have their eyes opened "in the breaking of the bread." When has the sacrament of communion revealed the divine presence to you? You might want to revisit the questions for the first chapter. Consider this question: As a pilgrim, have you heard Jesus' voice, felt Jesus' touch, or not? In what ways does this presence/absence beckon you forward?